T0368417

The Lost Voices of Children Never Heard

*A Minister & Professional Psychic Mediums
Perspective on Abortion*

Susan Rawlings

Balboa Press books may be ordered through booksellers or by contacting:

Balboa Press
A Division of Hay House
1663 Liberty Drive
Bloomington, IN 47403
www.balboapress.com
844-682-1282

ISBN: 979-8-7652-4361-9 (sc)
ISBN: 979-8-7652-4362-6 (e)

Library of Congress Control Number: 2023912537

Print information available on the last page.

Balboa Press rev. date: 11/27/2023

BALBOA.PRESS
A DIVISION OF HAY HOUSE

DISCLAIMERS

This book is not a substitute for Medical care or & Medical Mental Health advice. Please always consult your medical and or professional mental health counselor doctor about anything of a medical nature. I am not a medical Doctor I am a Professional Psychic Medium & Minister giving insight on a very controversial subject. Please always get proper medical advice from a qualified professional

I am not offering any opinions about what an individual chooses to do if there is an unwanted pregnancy that is an individual own personal choice that has nothing to do with me. I am not recommending termination that is a persons own individual choice to make on their own.

The content of this book are from my experiences only, I cannot speak on behalf of anyone I know, am related to or how other Psychic Mediums perceive this subject. Every Psychic Medium is different in their abilities. This book is strictly what I have learned over the nearly 30 years of being an Internationally known and a very well respected Psychic Medium and Christian Minister.

My deepest & sincere condolences to anyone who has ever lost a child no matter what the circumstances were surrounding the passing of your precious child.

Thank you for reading this information and keeping an open mind!

THANKS AND ACKNOWLEDGEMENT

I would like to thank all of the beautiful spirits who have come to communicate with me, and teach me about all of the information that I am sharing in this book. Also, for the beautiful messages of comfort that they were able to provide to their loved ones who were suffering emotionally because of difficult choices they more than likely did not want to make. I also deeply appreciate my dear husband Alexander, amazing colleagues, dear friends, clients that have become like family and all of my loved ones who have been so incredibly supportive and helpful to me through this process of my publishing journey. You all know who you are because I have reached out and thanked you personally, each and everyone of you. Some of the people who had the biggest impact on my life experience in a positive and inspirational way while they were alive are now living in spirit, I feel their presence daily, and I'm so grateful for the guidance on a divine level. Susan Rawlings

The Lost Voices of Children Never Heard -
A Professional Psychic Mediums Perspective on Abortion

Author: Reverend Susan Rawlings Internationally
known Professional Psychic Medium

CHAPTER I

Susan the Reverend & Professional Psychic Medium
The personal experiences prompted the publishing of this book

The sun had barely begun to rise when 22 year old Sarah trekked through the damp grass, a sign in one hand and the other tightly clutching that of her best friend's. They made their way toward the enraged cries of passionate protestors, all cumulatively fighting for the rights of women throughout the country .

"We won't go back" echoed throughout the crowd as raised signs swung atop the swarms of people. It was June 24, 2022, the day after Roe vs. Wade was overturned.

The United States has endured a tumultuous relationship with abortion rights spanning decades. Tangled in the violent ebb and flow of the American government, the issue at hand has been met with scrutiny and opposition. The issue itself has been at a stalemate, with no negotiation from either side of the political spectrum.

My intention of writing this book does not revolve around a political or religious agenda, although sometimes mentioned briefly. This book was strictly written due to a very unexpected series of experiences that happened in my career. I'm writing this book in an effort to advocate for women's rights and to educate those looking for answers of a higher divine nature.

As a Professional Psychic Medium and a Minister, I have gained insight into where those souls of the aborted fetuses go following an abortion. I feel as though it is my responsibility to share that with the rest of the world. It is also my great hope that the message I'm conveying will help others to have an open mind and try to look at such a controversial topic in an open minded light and compassionate light.

Life is expansive and multi-faceted, as is the after-life. As mere mortals, we have tunnel vision in the grand workings of the world, and that beyond which we can see. We aren't provided with a road map or a 360 degree aerial view. We're constantly seeking foregone conclusions in a world that's difficult to navigate. I was blessed with the gifts I was given and the opportunity to see beyond our own realm, and it is my duty to share my knowledge with others.

Born on the 19th of July in 1967 as Susan Elaine Stelz, I was one of the fortunate ones who made a grand entrance into this world with my third eye fully open. My earliest recollection of psychic mediumship traits started as an infant and began to exponentially grow throughout the years.

One day I was giving a dear friend of mine a reading. While I was in massage therapy school, I was giving a dear friend of mine a reading after she found out I was a Psychic and a Medium. Shortly after we graduated from Massage Therapy school, she started a beautiful spiritual bookstore and asked if I would help her run retail while the room in the back could be used for massage therapy clients. At the same time she was offering me this opportunity, she asked me if I would be interested in doing Psychic Mediumship readings and featured me as one of the house Psychic Mediums in her store! I accepted the position and that was the start of my Professional Psychic Mediumship career!

I was a single mother at the time with an expensive house payment. Within a span of 13 months of working at my friend's store, I was able to quit my day job and start running my business full-time, giving me more time to raise my son and enjoy his youth before it slipped away.

At the time I remember struggling with this decision; unsure that I wanted to be a professional Psychic Medium. However, the people that I worked for for 10 years had become like an extended family to me along with the loving members of our staff we all made great money, and all got along very well. Needless to say, I loved that job but knew it would be nothing but a dead end job for me although the money was excellent. To this day I still go to this place of business and visit my extended family whenever I can.

Changing times, Roe v. Wade then and now

In short, Roe V. Wade is a landmark Supreme Court decision that established a constitutional right to abortion. The ruling struck down laws in many states that had barred abortion, declaring that they could not ban the procedure before the point at which a fetus can survive outside the womb.

1973 United States Supreme Court case

Roe v. Wade, 410 U.S. 113 (1973), was a landmark decision of the U.S. Supreme Court in which the Court ruled that the Constitution of the United States protects a pregnant woman's liberty to choose to have an abortion without excessive government restriction. The decision struck down many U.S. federal and state abortion laws. wikipedia.org

Roe V. Wade was implemented on January 22, 1973 and was overturned June 2022. Who will be most impacted by this decision? What will happen if people can't access abortions?

The only alternative to abortion is childbirth, which has a 14 times higher risk of death than that of abortion. So, in denying a person access to a wanted abortion, states are forcing people to assume significant medical risk against their will. A recent study out of Colorado ominously predicts a significant rise in the maternal mortality rate. Statistics show especially among Black women who already experience an unacceptably high rate of death in childbearing. All women need to be safe and feel safe in their own bodies.

The Turn Away Study

The Turn Away Study is ANSIRH's prospective longitudinal study examining the effects of unwanted pregnancy on women's lives. The major aim of the study is to describe the mental health, physical health, and socioeconomic consequences of receiving an abortion compared to carrying an unwanted pregnancy to term. The main finding of The Turn Away Study is that receiving an abortion, in most cases, does not harm the health and wellbeing of women. In fact, being denied an abortion results in worse financial, health and family outcomes.

Research from the Turn Away study demonstrated other deleterious impacts of being denied a wanted abortion. This study followed ~1000 self-identified women for five years after receiving or being denied a wanted abortion. They found that denying these women an abortion creates economic hardship and insecurity that lasts for years. Compared with women who obtained their desired abortion, women denied the abortion had lowered credit scores as well as increased debt, bankruptcies, and evictions. Women turned away from getting an abortion were also more likely to stay in contact with a violent partner. The financial well-being and development of prior and subsequent children was also negatively impacted. Finally, giving birth was connected to more serious long-term health problems than having an abortion.

The Third Eye is and energy center that every human being has

The third eye (also called the mind's eye or inner eye) is a mystical invisible eye, usually depicted as located on the forehead, which provides perception beyond ordinary sight. the third eye is said to be located around the middle of the forehead, slightly above the junction of the eyebrows, representing the enlightenment one achieves through meditation. The third eye refers to the gate that leads to the inner realms and spaces of higher consciousness. In spirituality, the third eye often symbolizes a state of enlightenment. The third eye is often associated with religious visions, clairvoyance, the ability to observe chakras and auras, precognition, and out-of- body experiences. People who are said to have the capacity to use their third eyes are sometimes known as Seers, Psychics, Mediums.

I was born into a long lineage of psychic mediums, both on my maternal and paternal sides. As of today, I have been a Professional Psychic Medium for over 28 years at the time of this publication, bestowing my gifts upon those desperately seeking answers to provide them solace in whatever happens to be plaguing them at the time. Throughout my career, I've successful assisted police departments and detectives on numerous high-profile cases. I have an international following and thousands of clients throughout the world that rely heavily upon my readings. While this innate ability that I harbor runs through my bloodline, I am the first in this generation of my family to take my psychic capacities to a professional level.

There is a difference between a Psychic and a Medium. A Psychic is a person who can mentally travel throughout the passage of time and gather information that is beneficial to another human being. We now have the science and studies from the United States Military Remote Viewing program, developed for defense reasons in the Stargate Program Remote my Remote Viewing training was taken with a Best Selling author who was an original member of the Remote Viewing Military Stargate team where Remote Viewing was developed by the United States Military for defense purposes. Remote Viewing is a **scientifically** proven method to transcend time and space to psychically view anything past, present or future on or off planet person, place or thing and everyone in the class was successful on the first try!

I have the instinctive gift to not only see future events that have yet to occur, but I can see prolific events from a person's past that have had a significant impact on their lives. Oftentimes, they're unaware of the power this specific event has held over them. In a lot of cases, their subconscious has blocked them from detecting the influence that such an event has had on their daily lives. They were unaware that they have been standing in their own way.

On many occasions, the person I'm reading for isn't always aware they've been standing in their own way. I have the innate ability to get beyond their subconscious and break the impenetrable walls that are looming in front of them. When I go into mediumship and reading mode, and evolve into a trans-like state, I am walking between two worlds as I gather my intel for whomever is sitting before me.

Aside from my psychic abilities, I am also a Medium. Some people are gifted solely with psychic abilities or mediumship abilities. I happen to be born with both abilities. Mediumship is my ability to speak to loved ones that have passed over to the other side that belong to my clientele. This part of my job is the most rewarding part of anything else I do. It's as if I get to spend a part of my day in Heaven, which is a state of eternal bliss.

I have been seeing spirits since I was a young child. Initially, I didn't have the maturity or the understanding to thoroughly comprehend what it was I was experiencing. One of my first recollections of mediumship was being in the children's choir at my local church and seeing angels all around me. Being young and naïve, I assumed they were members of the congregation. It wasn't until I was older and began working with several wise, experienced spiritual mentors that have guided me over the years that I understood that I am also a Medium. What I had been directly experiencing for years were the presence of actual Spirits, Angels, Gods and Goddess, Deities basically the essence of anything alive. The essence of our soul is an eternal life force.

In regard to the physical form a soul that has passed on takes, the vast majority of the time they are presented in the same form as they did when they were living. If the pregnancy was terminated, they show up in the form of what they would have looked like and personality characteristics that they would have demonstrated. Some souls appear as older or younger, but will always show themselves to me in a way that a client can identify who the spirit is talking to from were they now reside. They will provide pertinent information about themselves from when they were a physical presence in this world and their correlation to the client. If the soul was not able to incarnate due to a termination, they will tell me all about who they were, what they looked like, even names that they would have liked to have been named. Many of my clients verified the names they had picked out for children that they may have had in mind for a male or female child and verified my accuracy. Any time a soul comes forth in a person's reading, it means they've been overseeing the well-being of their loved one, and are more than likely serving as a guardian angel to the person I am reading for.

From what I have learned through all or my years of experience, our angels are not to interfere with our free will. They can give us gentle nudges in the right direction unless it involves a life-or-death situation, and the person has a strong reason to remain on this planet. This is a way to have more open communication with your loved ones on the other side by giving them permission to interfere with your free will. Trust me, they know what is best for us and I have learned over the years that if I don't listen to my angels, I will live to regret it. At this point in my life, I have allowed everyone I know from the other side that will come around me to interfere with my free will for what is for my best for my long term happiness, prosperity, good health and all good things moving forward for myself and the world around me. I now have so many opportunities that I am struggling to see which one will be the most profitable. That is definitely not a complaint. It is a blessing that has helped me tremendously. I hope that if you decide to try this exercise, it will work for you as well!

There is one important loophole I have learned in the last 3 years due to the turmoil on this planet. The divine essence is allows humans to have more interaction with the other side. I recommend giving any angel or deceased loved one permission to interfere with all good things that will provide you assistance in everything you may need to have a great life and protection. I have been doing this for the last three years and because of these connections that I have created on a much deeper level with all of my loved ones that have crossed over, I have so many doors open career wise that I don't even know which one to pick! That is how they have helped me.

I always explain this to my clients and ask if they are comfortable enough with assigning their loved ones on a permanent basis, and to this day not one client has ever said no! I ask them to partake in a small exercise with me. I have them close their eyes and envision their loved one, or several, that have passed on. I have them either think or say along with me "I give you complete permission to interfere with my free will for what is best for myself, my family and my loved ones, and the world around me."

Once I began teaching this method, I received incredible feedback from my clients. The clients would consistently reach out and tell me how doors have been opening up for them effortlessly. In my opinion, this is attributed to them giving their permission to their angels to guide them in the best direction possible. Once permission was granted, their angels would immediately go to work for them and steer them in the right direction. YOU have to be the person to get up and take the opportunities or let them pass by. This leaves us with a lot of personal responsibility for taking action and believing in yourself. I would not be shown these things if the client weren't capable of it. There is a level of ethics that you have to follow. You may have to be willing to challenge yourself out of your comfort zone to grow to your fullest potential. The angels will get very frustrated if you are a lazy person not reaching your fullest potential. We all came here to learn lessons to strengthen our souls.

There's a frenzied yearning brought forth by my clients as they make their way through the threshold of my office; a thirst for the instantaneous answers and full-thought out solutions to their issues at hand. Toward the end of their sessions, it's as if they're an entirely different person. One of my great joys in life is seeing the transformation; one of solace, peace and overall relief. That chaos and confusion had dissipated throughout the hour and have been met with a sense of harmony.

These gifts that I possess came from a power greater than myself, and not even necessarily *someone*. I am just a vessel for divine messages. All I know is that I have absolutely no control whether or not the sun rises every morning or which way the wind will blow. But with my gifts, I am able to offer some semblance and purpose to those on the search for answers they are so desperate to find. I wish I had answers as to why people suffer or why the world works the way it does. But not a single soul on the planet has those answers. What I have is the ability to provide guidance and a roadmap to help them reach their optimal life purpose.

I only know myself as a Psychic-Medium because I was born that way. I do not understand life without my abilities. I have always loved possessing these gifts. I had so much fun with my abilities as a child and was able to take these gifts and turn them into a profession.

CHAPTER II

Q. Roe v Wade has been overturned. What will happen now across the country?

A. Nine states have already implemented their abortion bans. Another dozen states are in the process. Legal chaos is occurring as injunctions against individual state laws are being lifted and pre-Roe bans are being interpreted. In a few states, new injunctions are being issued before laws can go into effect. Governors who are hostile to abortion, but whose states have not yet fully banned abortion, are contemplating whether to call special sessions of the legislature to consider new abortion bans.

Abortion providers in all the banned and several of the in-process states have stopped providing abortion care or reduced the type of care they offer. People with previously scheduled appointments are scrambling to find new appointments in states where some abortion is still available. These include abortion-safe states, as well as states like Florida, Ohio, and Georgia where there are new gestational limits for abortion, but not yet complete bans.

Abortion clinics in states where abortion remains legal, including Illinois and Kansas, are working hard to expand appointment availability by hiring new staff, increasing the physical plant of their facilities, and adding additional clinic appointments. Clinics in the in-process states are doing their best to manage immediate increased patient demand, even as they are preparing for a future in which they may not be able to continue offering abortions.

Who will be most impacted by this decision?
What will happen if people can't access abortions?

The only alternative to abortion is childbirth, which has a **14 times higher risk of death** than that of abortion. Therefore, in denying a person access to a wanted abortion, states are forcing people to assume significant medical risk against their will. A recent study out of Colorado ominously predicts a significant rise in the maternal mortality rate, especially among Black women who already experience an unacceptably high rate of death in childbearing.

Research from the Turn Away study demonstrated other deleterious impacts of being denied a wanted abortion. This study followed ~1000 self-identified women for five years after receiving or being denied a wanted abortion. They found that denying these women an abortion creates economic hardship and insecurity that lasts for years. Compared with women who obtained their desired abortion, women denied the abortion had lowered credit scores as well as increased debt, bankruptcies, and evictions. Women turned away from getting an abortion were also more likely to stay in contact with a violent partner. The financial well-being and development of prior and subsequent children was also negatively impacted. Finally, giving birth was connected to more serious long-term health problems than having an abortion.

I would never have thought in a million years that I would be writing about such a controversial topic as abortion laws. The reasoning behind this is due to the importance of sharing a Psychic Medium's and minister's prospective on abortion which is a much different view now that I have had these experiences through the experience with my clients. With the laws changing and women's rights in jeopardy, it is vital that I share what I know with whomever is seeking answers. It is my personal opinion that the governmental establishment has absolutely no right to dictate what women can and cannot do with their own bodies.

Birth control isn't always a reliable guarantee. I am, in fact, an IUD baby. I was conceived, as was my brother, while the woman who gave birth to me was using an Inter Uterine Device to prevent pregnancy. Having memories of my infancy from the time of being born is not a common occurrence. However, I can vividly remember life from a very young age. Not everything of course, yet very vivid memories. Although I was an infant and unable to obtain an understanding of the physical world, I was still connected to the spiritual world. This provided me with the conscious awareness of my surroundings.

My point in bringing this up is that the vast majority of the human population cannot grasp the idea that infants can understand the world around them. They are cognizant of more than we give them credit for. And although infants live in the physical world, they also inhabit the spiritual world until they develop at a certain age. Their presence on two different plains serves as a mechanism to protect them. This dynamic will continue for at least the first two years of the child's life until the fontanelle (sometimes referred to as the soft spot on the top of the infant's skull) however most children remain very open to the spirit world until the age of six or seven.

While the fetus itself may be inhabiting the womb of a pregnant woman, it is simultaneously taking up residence in the spiritual realm until it is fully developed enough to inhabit this world in its entirety.

One of my strongest memories as a new born infant was of the the mother figure to me and she was holding me in her arms and rocking me in a chair. Although my higher self knew she loved me, I was also vastly aware that she did not want to take care of me and that I would have to raise myself and it was probably going to be a difficult dynamic. Six and a half years later with an IUD in another child was conceived my younger brother who I adore. I acknowledge the fact that raising four children was hard, and even more difficult was having two that were unplanned.

Regardless, I could've chosen to go about my life harboring a victim's mentality, or I could live a life in strength and independence.

As I have been going through the process of writing this book, several questions, come to mind one especially now that abortions are being outlawed in certain parts of the United States. Will birth control be outlawed in the United States?

Yes, birth control remains legal everywhere in the United States, though several states allow doctors and pharmacists to refuse to prescribe or dispense contraceptives. According to the Guttmacher Institute. The Supreme Court decision overturning Roe v. Wade does not indicate that the court would revisit past decisions about birth control.

However, some legal experts have raised concerns that justices could apply the argument for overturning Roe to limiting access to contraceptives. As a result, those who support birth control access worry that legislators could use a ban on abortion to make birth control less available.

"We've seen folks falsely equating emergency contraceptives and IUDs with abortion," said straight from the director of birth control access and senior counsel at the National Women's Law Center gave a statement quoting "That's certainly something I'm concerned about." Meaning that this director more than likely is concerned that the next thing to be outlawed could possibly be birth control. Although, I seriously doubt that will ever happen if this information is coming from the director of The National Women's Law Center. We may want to pay more attention to the possibility of birth control laws being vulnerable to attack as well.

One concern that has been raised is whether laws, like one in Oklahoma, that ban abortion from the moment of fertilization would also outlaw intrauterine devices, or IUDs, which are designed to prevent fertilization, but also can stop a fertilized egg from implanting in the uterus. (The Oklahoma law specifies that it does not apply to contraception, including Plan B or morning-after pills.)

From my observation and personal experiences, the dynamic between the woman who gave birth to me and my brother was entirely different than that of my own relationship with her. I was the third of three girls, and he was the token male, which was not his choice. I vividly recall the day my parents were giving us the news that they were expecting another child in our family. The mother figure to me at the time was alternating between hair-raising screams and desperate cries while slamming pots and pans on the stove.

This woman had only wanted two children, which all were planned from what I was told. The mother figure to me was once a very beautiful, vibrant, funny, talented and super intellectual woman. I always felt that she was a woman who desired to have a career. Given that this was the early 1970s and women in the workplace was a societal norm, a career wasn't something that would have necessarily been out of reach. But when I, the uninvited family member was born, my mother figure's hopes for obtaining a career were dashed. At least in her eyes. The financial burden instead fell upon my father, providing for a family of six on one income.

As a child, my needs were ultimately rejected by the mother figure to me. This big eyed, curly haired little girl had absolutely no effect on her whatsoever. While my other siblings had been enrolled in various activities that instilled self-confidence in them that I was not privy to, I was left waiting in the wings, undeserving of participating. I was constantly reminded by an immediate family member that my life was considered to be a complete mistake because the birth control had failed. I was reminded on many occasions that I remember being told that I was a "mistake" rather than a "surprise"

I was constantly being compared to my siblings that had a way better chance than me starting off in early life. They were involved in cheerleading, gymnastics, Girl Scouts, ceramics lesson, knitting lessons! I was told often that I wasn't smart enough, skinny enough or as pretty as my sisters were, leaving my confidence level waning. As both a child and a woman, I have always been a bit curvier than my petite siblings. This led to constant taunting and the inability to fit into their hand-me-down clothing, except for shoes. This woman was constantly implying that I was too fat, even to the point of putting me in a constant states of humiliation by imposing food portion restrictions on me. There was also the constant threat of getting the silent treatment for months at a time. One can only imagine the torment that would cause a young woman in her formidable years.

This mother figure was so mad at me in my early formative years that she decided to not speak to me for months after she read my diary, which was nothing but a compilation of day to day things that any normal teenager would feel. One day I wrote in there that I hated my mother and in another passage I wrote that on that particular day I couldn't stand my brother. In my opinion, those are normal teenager experiences. I was threatened with the embarrassment of the mother figure reading all of my private thoughts to everyone in our family until my father for the first time intervened because he knew she had literally broken my spirit.

Luckily my dear sweet amazing father and I developed a deep connection with one another as he was the more dominant parental figure in my life. He had always wanted six children, when his wife had only wanted two. The divine essence brought them together to meet in the middle with four children.

My father had served his country in the Air Force and went on to work a full-time job while enrolled in college, while simultaneously providing for his family. I remember my father's college graduation just like it was yesterday even though I was about 4 years of age. All of us have REAL smiles plastered across our faces in all of the pictures that were taken that day, as we took so much pride in his graduation and the fact that we got to spend the day with our Grandparents that we rarely were allowed to see.

My father always took the time to play with us. Even though his life was so busy, even when he was working full time and going to college full time he still found some way to fit us in his busy schedule. Immediately after he graduated, he bought land and built a beautiful home in the country for all of us to live in. I remember as a young student struggling with math. Although he was so busy and had so much work to do, he wouldn't hesitate to help me with my homework that I was struggling with.

He always took my female siblings and I camping, bike riding, cave hunting, taught us how to live off of the land, and we always had a blast fishing at my favorite aunt and uncle's farm that had a huge pond on the land. Since he raised us on a farm, he taught us how to live off the land. We became amazing in gardening and farming, learning how to raise animals and chop wood in the summertime so that we could stay warm in the winter months. I ended up becoming a tomboy with my dad because deep down, I knew he wanted a boy. So, I did everything I could to try to keep up with doing things a boy would do. I appreciate that aspect of my relationship with my father as it helped me acquire a strong work ethic and taught me independence and how to live off the land. The most important thing he taught me was **unconditional love,** so did my paternal grandparents, aunt and uncle.

During her pregnancy with my brother, the mother figure became extremely depressed. I also wonder looking back if there were some undiagnosed post partum depression. The depression continued to grow even after he was born, which is why it was out of sorts that he would become her favorite child. He grew uncomfortable of obtaining the "golden child" status, so much so that, in my opinion, he and my sister-in-law moved out of state, halfway across the United States to escape the firm grasp my mother figure has upon him. That was only my observation and opinion of the move and I have never even discussed that with him. I was just happy for him that he was far away, although I didn't get to see him as much and miss him and my sweet sister-in-law so much.

As I was growing up, I noticed that my mother figure never wanted to let my sweet brother get his hands dirty. Living on a farm makes that a fairly challenging feat. She would barely let him leave the house when there was outdoor work to be done. Because of this dynamic, when the weather was permitting we would spend so much time together and ended up creating a very deep bond. From what I observed, our mother figure used fear mongering techniques on my him, often convincing him that his allergies were too bad to break through the threshold of the front door. My brother and I have cultivated a special bond in our adult lives.

My brother a funny no nonsense kind of guy and has opened up about a few times expressing the awkwardness he was experiencing at times with the dynamic, yet still loves and is very close to the mother figure. I am so happy for him that he got the support from a mother figure that was way more positive than mine was over the years. He shared how he would woefully watch my father and I outside while our mother figure kept him within her grasp and forced him to stay indoors, wishing he could be out there with us because we were always having so much fun.

I want to express that I have the vast understanding that some people have deeper connections with others because they recognize them as part of their soul family. I understand that my mother figure had this instant connection with my brother. However, choosing a favorite child can be a detriment to the other children and to the favored child in a family. I have watched this dynamic play out for a lifetime and and now at 56 years of age, and trust me it is an awful feeling and for the most part has been a nightmare.

I hold no resentment toward that situation, although it is still playing out. I am now completely estranged from everyone expect for a few dear family members because the others are afraid of acknowledging the horribly uncomfortable truth. I had this kind of connection with my father's mother & father, my sweet grandmother, Peggy & Grandpa Ray. It was just something that happened the connection was deep immediately. They protected me and loved me unconditionally. Their home was the only place as a child I remember being at peace and able to be my true self. My mother figure's disdain for me became so apparent to others that several adults talked openly about it to me in a loving way and help me understand this was not a normal dynamic, even my sweet, paternal grandparents, who never said anything bad about either of our parents. Thank God my sweet Grandma pulled me aside on several occasions, wanting to discuss what they saw unfolding before their eyes. They never once said anything negative about my mother figure, and Grandma Peggy used to always say "this dynamic is not the way life is supposed to be and someday you will grow up and not have to deal with this. I love you Suzy." Suzy was my childhood name.

Due to the fact I was so empathic and was able to feel everything, the emotional despair I was experiencing was completely confusing and not ready for the real world. Because of this, I coped by forming self-destructive behaviors - alcoholism. It was my choice to take that first drink, I take complete responsibility for my actions, and continued drinking until I was able to defeat my metaphorical dragon. Therefore, I developed a drinking problem in my teens. I was labeled as "Sensitive Suzy," as I was unable to decipher one minute from the next, or be able to identify what emotion was mine or if I was empathizing with someone else. Of course not all psychics have this problem. However, a lot of psychics are so sensitive that they end up finding various ways to self-medicate. Psychics can also become very overwhelmed and have intense anxiety issues. It took a while, but I finally found the guidance I needed and no longer had a need to self medicate through difficult emotional situations.

Due to this emotional abuse and disconnect with my mother figure as a young child, I quickly learned how to disassociate. A lot of my psychic colleagues have had traumatic childhoods, which helped enhance their abilities as psychics exactly the way I did. Part of the reason why we are so good at what we do is because we learned at a very young age how to disassociate from our bodies and let our souls hang out in the energy field. It must be part of the journey that some psychics need to go through to reach their full potential. I am not implying that all Psychics and Mediums have a difficult upbringing. I am only expressing that the majority of Psychics & Mediums that I know have had a lot of trauma in life that in some odd way caused the majority of us to easily disassociate which allows us access to Psychic information.

CHAPTER III

The Hair Salon
How I was inspired to write this book and why

The pinnacle time in my life that drew me to writing this book unfolded as a true story in my own past. At one point in my career, I had achieved a level of success that led me to upgrading my office. I wanted a more appealing aesthetic for my clients to be immersed in. As I began my search for a new, more conducive office, I was drawn to a quaint three-story brick building. It was on a busy street in the capital city of the state I live in. I was given an office on the first floor, complete with a beautiful porch and a separate entrance. At the time it was quite a step up, as I was paying $800 a month for office rent.

The building was formerly occupied by a very prominent religious organization and had since been transformed into a hair salon and I was doing readings there as well. One of the people who rented space from me started doing some digging and discovered that the office right next door to my office was where people from the religious organization would gather and pray for the souls of the aborted children. I was astounded! Clarity instantaneously came over me and it became clear as to why I was picking up on this topic like I never had before. My reasoning behind planting my business in the midst of a salon was my assessment that I would acquire more business, which ended up becoming a reality. One day, the owner of the business approached me, inquiring if I could take over the salon, due to financial burdens she was facing. I have to look back and laugh at myself as I knew absolutely nothing about the cosmetic industry. But I wanted my business to remain in that specific building.

After a few months of negotiation with the business owner, I ended up taking over the entire business. Due to the fact that the clientele coming for beauty services also had great recommendations from my colleagues in the beauty industry, it ended up becoming a great fit. After an aesthetician that I admired favored my office that I was occupying at the time, I agreed to moving my office on the second floor. This new office, although in the same building is where I began picking up psychically & through mediumship abilities on almost every woman who had terminated a pregnancy.

Although my office on the top floor didn't have a charming porch and its own separate entrance, it had a very comfortable feel to it. I truly did love it. However, shortly after moving to that floor was when I began to have these unusual occurrences take place. Unfamiliar messages started coming through, which truly made me uncomfortable at the time. I was able to pick up on every female that had come into my office that had previously terminated a pregnancy. I had the ability to identify the soul of the child that had been terminated and one by one, the souls of these children had absolutely no animosity toward their parents, which was a surprise to me.

I began to let some of my clients & colleagues know what I was experiencing. I found a way to gently inform the client as to what was occurring. Might I add, it wasn't only the female clients I had picked up on, but the male clients who were the paternal figure in these aborted pregnancies. Rather than straight up declare 'I know that you had an abortion.' I settled upon a more subtle approach by very kindly asking their permission to talk about a very sensitive topic and they all said YES, they did not want me to hold back any information. I had no intention of embarrassing or shaming someone. My heart is filled with compassion because I could sense the despair. I simply wanted to impart the knowledge I had acquired and it turned into an entire experience worth writing about!

I delicately informed my clients that I was in contact with these souls that have never made it into physical incarnation. This seemed to have been a beneficial message toward some kind of emotional relief or resolution to a lifelong burden these people endured and they ended up thanking me; both men and women. The women or men would start an open discussion about the experience they had endured. I could not believe the amount of comforting messages that were being exchanged. I would relay the message from the soul of the child to the parent, and every time this exchange was made, all the pent-up guilt and remorse would dissipate. I could see the pure relief come over the faces of these people almost like a liberating freedom. I even went from buying one box of tissues for my office that I had to start buying tissues in bulk packages.

The souls of the aborted children also made it known that there was a significant amount of souls waiting to incarnate on the earth, and that the concept of ending a pregnancy was decided by the divine essence and the parental units of the spirit of the child. The children wanted to relay the message that they understood what had happened and that the earth was not the easiest place to not only live in, but to evolve in. They held the knowledge that the cosmos of life on earth is considered one of the most difficult to be immersed in.

These souls wanted me to transmit the message that they would make a valiant attempt to become a part of either of their parents' lives; both mother and father if possible. This would be done by incarnating as another child, or somewhere in the immediate family; niece, nephew, grandchild, etc. They always remained close in the energy field of the mother, serving as an angel from the other side to help their parents' lives if reincarnation was not an option. I see this a lot with godparents and even adoptions. These souls are always close in the energy field of the mother or father. In fact, I have a child currently in my life that I did not give birth to, but consider her to be my daughter, although we share no blood relation. If anything ever happened to her mother, I would take her in and adopt her, making her my own. I believe this girl is a huge part of my soul family. So is my sweet stepson Keith who is like a biological son to me. Although I did not give birth to him, I love him like I did give birth to him!

It's of the upmost importance to relay that the souls of these terminated children were never upset with the parents. I have never gotten a connection from a child soul that was a late term abortion, so it is not my place to touch on that subject. In my opinion, the only time a late term abortion is acceptable is if the mother's health is in jeopardy. But in all other circumstances, these aborted souls always want to come back and reincarnate with the mother or families by any means, they want to be reunited into the soul circle when the time was right.

The prayers that were bestowed upon the souls of the children from the Religious Foundation were always extremely valued and appreciated from the other side. However, the children questioned the lack of prayers directed toward the well-being of their mothers or fathers and the difficult decision they felt they had no other choice but to make.

As this journey continued on, and so many of the women and men heard from the soul of their child, a state of solace and contentment permeated throughout the room as I revealed how their lost child truly felt about them. I would regale them in stories all about their child; what they looked like, their personal items, and on some occasion I had the ability to reveal the name that the parents would've bestowed upon them. Nearly every time I provided a name, they validated that the specific name I had revealed was in-fact the name that would've been given to the child.

After enduring such a shocking revelation, one of my beautiful clients suggested I pen a book based around this topic. For years she had been in an all-consuming state of trauma, encompassed by a ferocious cycle of unrelenting guilt and despair. As of today, the subject has been on the back burner for nearly seven years.

The mothers to the aborted souls informed me that they finally felt as though they could move forward in life without carrying all of the heavy baggage. The guilt had plagued them so much that it sabotaged their daily life and their self-worth. They had replaced their feelings with peace, understanding and happiness to know that they not only still had access to the soul of the child, but that the child was living in harmony.

Testimonials

Please note that all testimonials given in this book were unsolicited and to protect the privacy of my clients I have used different names. I tried to chose testimonials that would relate to what I learned though this very unexpected experiences.

Paula

"Susan, you have changed my life with your beautiful messages from my children. At the time I was young and did not want my boyfriend with so much potential to be held back from being the successful man that he is now. Your message has soothed both mine and my husbands hearts about a very difficult decision we had to make when we were young. Our hearts are much lighter now! You also verified just as I had suspected that my boys came back at the right time. As soon as both of them were born, I knew their souls so did my husband"

Nina

"I had never told anyone about my choice and Susan picked it up right away that I had been broken hearted about terminating a pregnancy as young girl. My decision was made not because I didn't want my baby, I was terrified of how my parents would react because I was still a teenager. I kept all of the guilt and sadness pent up inside of me for years suffering in silence. The reading that Susan gave me took away years of deep pain that I never thought would go away"

Tiffany

"I was once a drug addict and found myself pregnant, I was so selfish I was not ready to give up my drug habit so I terminated the pregnancy. Although these problems were self created I still have a heart and have never been able to forgive myself for being so weak. You have no idea the relief that you have given me!"

At the time drug addiction and a alcoholism were not considered a disease so people who had problems like this were very looked down upon as people who cannot control themselves. She is now clean and sober with 1 beautiful little boy and another little girl that came back to her when she was capable of raising them! I am so proud of her!

Danielle

"Susan picked up on my baby boy that never made it through due to unfortunate circumstances at the time there was no way I could handle a baby on my own, I knew the father would not help physically or financially. I had to make the unfortunate choice to terminate the pregnancy. A few years after this happened my brother was shot and killed causing our entire family to go into chaos. We stay in chaos for 2 years until my baby boy was born that was an exact image, personality traits just like my brother who was killed. Our entire family thought this baby could be my brother because of the strong resemblance and Susan verified for me that I was actually raising my brother who wanted a better chance this time so he picked his sister (me) to be his mother" This message changed our entire families outlook on life, we all have that sparkle back in our eyes"

John

"Many years ago my girlfriend had an abortion and I had no say in it, I even offered to raise the child on my own with no child support commitment from her. She wanted nothing to do with it and went to the clinic on her own for the procedure, I was devastated! Now that I have talked with Susan and she had no way of knowing this had happened to me in my youth I feel many years of burden leaving me with a peaceful understanding"

David

"I love children, Susan how did you know that I had one child that did not make it into incarnation?"

My response, I can see the child in your energy field except they don't come to me looking as infants usually the show themselves to me at about the age of 18-25 years of age and what they would have looked like and personality they would have embraced. He said I was raised Catholic and was convinced I had better live my best life now because I am for sure going to hell because of this decision" I assured him that his daughter understood, she loved him unconditionally, and would eventually come back into in life as a grandchild. A few years later I saw him and was so happy to sit with him and look at all of his pictures of his daughter/ granddaughter that had come back through one of his children. The connection this man had with this little girl was unshakable and he said he felt like he was actually living happily with no burdens and hadn't felt more positive about life in years"

Sonya

"My boyfriend and I were in Medical School together and loved my boyfriend, one day I found out I was with child. Obviously we were no were near ready to be parents so we decided together to never tell anyone because we were both so ashamed about this decision. After they were finished with school and all internships they were married and ready to become parents and start their awesome careers saving lives as doctors! That is exactly what happened, her first child was a little girl and this woman knew by looking in her daughters eyes that she had come back to us! She and her sibling are our world, thank you for giving us some peace of mind and understanding"

Rosemary

This particular experience was quite different than the others. This woman came into my office in her early 80s. I picked up the spirit of her child that wanted to talk to Rosemary. At the time Rosemary received her procedure, it was not legal. She had to have it done at someone's home the old fashion way, which we all know can turn out to be life-threatening. This is exactly what happened to this poor young woman. After her procedure, she received a terrible infection and ended up losing her uterus and could never have children again. She had blamed herself because she had made that decision and thought that it was Divine punishment to her for doing what she had done, especially back in that day, when things were not nearly as liberal as they are now.

She ended up being a schoolteacher because of this experience, and decided that since she could not have children of her own, that she would take care of everyone else's children. The soul of her child told me how proud she was of her mother, she went on to become the most loved and best teachers in the entire community. She was actually very reserved when I brought up the topic but I explained to her because she was worried what I might think about her. I told her that her child is so proud of her for taking care of everyone else's child and it had made the world a better place. She left my office with a huge smile.

CHAPTER IV

Soul Entrance into the Physical Body & Abortion

The souls of the children will enter the body directly before the mother is ready to give birth. The moment the child takes its first breath, or shortly thereafter, is when the soul and body become one entity. Due to the lapse of time in those nine months of gestation, it is a rather pointless pursuit to confine a soul to an enclosed space, so they usually will stay in the mother's energy field that is sometimes referred to as an aura until birth or shortly after their grand entrance into the world.

Many years ago, my body was under medical duress, so I underwent a hysterectomy. I have one son and gave birth to him naturally. At the time, epidurals were not offered, regardless of the fact they had been available for quite some time prior to my pregnancy. They had only been readily available for women with the financial means to procure them. Therefore I was never bestowed such an option. Based on my audible observance, most of the women that were giving birth that day were not offered epidurals either. The sounds of the pains of labor reverberated throughout the hallways. Based on what I was taking in, my labor was rather easy in comparison.

The actual hysterectomy surgery went fine. However, I did run into some risk during aftercare at the hospital, leading to a seven day stay. My doctor was not at fault. I had no ill-will against my doctor and had no intention of filing a lawsuit. My pain medication had been mixed up, and as a result of this mistake, my body went into complete shock twice within a four hour period. This resulted in a trauma team rushing into my room to resuscitate me twice. It ended up being a celestially beautiful experience as I had come upon what is referred to as an exit point. We all have them in our astrology charts. If life gets too difficult, we can make a choice to leave at a certain time, or we can choose to remain living. I chose to get back into my body and continue upon the path that was intended for my life with the help of my sweet Grandpa that came to greet me during both occurrences. I had the profound knowledge that there was too much work left to be done in my life. My grandfather Ray from the other side told me that I could either come with him or he could help me get back into my body. Both times I was in a tunnel of light with my grandfather. It was the most beautiful feeling of unconditional love, safety, peace and comfort that I had ever felt. The entire following year, I had experienced grave depression, having been thrown back into the negativity of day-to-day earth life.

Not everyone carries out their lives going through the motions on a day-to-day basis. However, at the time, that's how my life was. I was in a very ill-fated marriage. In addition to the emotional taxation, my husband was taking advantage of me financially, which eventually took a turn for the worst. I finally ended up filing for divorce and closing the curtain on that toxic relationship.

The year following my recovery, my depression persisted. It's difficult to aptly describe the effect of being immersed in the unconditional love from my grandfather and whatever light source energy that accompanied him, but it was pure, unequivocal love. Because of that experience, I welcome the day that I get to come back home after my work here on earth is done.

The emotional toll that was a result of my hysterectomy came with a silver lining. The seven days in the hospital following my surgery transformed into a beautiful experience because I had the opportunity to observe the babies coming in and out of the hospital. During my time confined between the walls of the hospital, I was able to kill time and walk around the hallways. It brought me great joy to observe the newborn babies.

By the time the babies made their way to the nursery, it appeared as though most of them had fully come into their bodies. However, some showed evidence that they were going through a process of integration. The process of integration appeared to be a part of the soul of the child hanging around the baby's body; partially here on earth, yet simultaneously holding on to the other side. It seemed as though it took some souls an approximated time of 24 hours after birth for the ones still hanging on to the other side to fully come into integration with their physical form. I was able to confirm years later once I was able to start communicating with the souls of the lost children that this indeed was true.

Even when I do readings for pregnant women, the soul of the child is always hanging around the mother's energy field right up until birth; right before they take their first breath. During this time, they can telepathically communicate with their mothers, even revealing to them what name they prefer to be called and what they'll be good at in life. To this day, I cannot remember ever having read for a pregnant woman where I saw the soul of the child's soul inside the womb during pregnancy. I could only see the fetus. Although the soul of the child has not yet come into the physical body, they always hang around in the mother's energy field with the intention of watching over her.

Due to my enhanced abilities that I was born with, I've been able to witness the entire process of soul integration, and I do not attribute it to mere happenstance. I believe that my seven day stay in the hospital was divinely lead so that I would have access to a nursery as a learning opportunity. Based on my observations, I was able to learn from the souls of the children that if there is an abortion procedure executed, the soul of the child has not yet been integrated.

I was brought up in the Christian church and to this day hold my minister's license. This provided me with a strong foundation for religion and for that I was grateful to have experienced. Christianity, it gave me a wonderful foundation to build my own divine belief system upon. Currently I am going through a 4 year study with a very respectable Magickal organization that is held in very high regard globally, and eventually will be trading in my minister's license for my Pagan minister's license. As soon as I am finished with my formal training, I will be considered a High Priestess .

Although in adult life, I chose to go down a few alternative paths of religion that made more sense to me and provided me with a comfort that Christianity did not as I grew on my own spiritual path. I do not in any way consider abortion to be a sin. It is a choice that no one should ever judge. My ministers never taught me to be judgmental. They encouraged me to learn how to love unconditionally. The topic of abortion was never even discussed in our church. I hope this book will give humanity a different perspective and an alternative outlook at such a taboo topic that's seen a drastic increase in public discussion. There aren't many psychics out there that would be willing to put 28 years of their career on the line to write a book as controversial as this one.

From the result of my research, it is estimated that one in four pregnancies end in abortion and a much higher percentage rate of humanity somewhere around the 70% plus range believe that abortion should be legal.

As I continue to share this information with women who have been through the tragic experience of having to make such a difficult choice, I am met with an abundance of gratitude and appreciation. There was a sense of solace that accompanied acquiring this information, as there has always been a religious controversy centered around abortion, stating such an act as sinful and those that partook in such a sinful, appalling act are destined for an eternity of hellfire and brimstone, which is so far from the truth as I know it.

My intention of explaining the process of how and when the soul enters the body right before the baby takes its first breath is to provide a comforting message. To anyone who has spent days, months, or years carrying around guilt, fear and shame, you are all beautiful people that, unfortunately at some point in your life journey were faced with a challenging decision. In my 28 years as a professional psychic-medium, I have never seen the soul of a woman be sentenced to Hell for choosing to have an abortion.

CHAPTER V

A Psychic Mediums & Ministers perspective on Miscarriages

My deepest & sincere condolences to anyone who has ever lost a child, no matter what the circumstances were surrounding the passing of your precious child.

Please understand that I was very hesitant about writing a chapter about miscarriages & SIDS in the same book addressing this controversial topic of because I would never want to offend any woman who has had a miscarriage, the loss of a child, Sudden Infant Death Syndrome especially by expressing experiences personally and through the readings of my clients. My hopes in writing about these topic from a Psychic perspective is that the messages will be comforting to anyone who has ever lost a child no matter what the circumstances are.

However, I have a lot of Psychic insight and in a book that is primarily focused on a psychic's perspective of abortion. I decided it was an important topic to touch on these subjects as well, due to tragic experience that unfolded in my life many years ago; an unexpected miscarriage.

At the time of this occurrence, I was a single mother working two jobs to make ends meet. I had my one sweet incredible son who was born with a lot of health issues that were very hard on him. Due to the attention his medical issues required, I had no intention of bringing another child into this world at that time. My son, who was such an incredible fighting champ no matter what health issues he had made him more determined to succeed in life. Up until the age of 13 years, he needed all my attention and there wasn't any other way around it. Due to the severity of his health issues, it was even difficult for me to find childcare. We were both so blessed that the beautiful hearted family members at the time came to our aid. My son lived with me full-time, yet spent a lot of time with family when I was at work.

One day out of the blue, I began severely hemorrhaging. It became so critical that I was soaking entire bath towels full of blood. When I finally made it to the emergency room and was able to see a doctor, he explained that I was having a miscarriage. This came as a complete shock to me because at the time, I had no idea I was even pregnant. I had not been unable to take birth control as it made me sick, and the man that I was in a long-term relationship with was well aware of that fact. At the time we were engaged, so I thought he would be my future husband and I loved him dearly.

Although at the time I truly loved that man, he handled the situation in a less than respectable manner. In fact, his behavior was beyond hurtful and beyond insensitive. I needed a ride to the hospital in the midst of everything and since I didn't have health insurance at the time, calling an ambulance was out of the question. I had no other option but to call him. I didn't feel it would be safe driving in that condition with my son in the car. This man had a demanding job so reluctantly left work to take me to the hospital. However, I was astounded when he dropped me off at the doors to the emergency room and sped off. I was left alone and terrified without the slightest understanding as to what was taking place. Shortly after the miscarriage, our relationship completely fell apart, thank God. For understandable reasons I was able to see his true nature before I made a huge mistake by marrying him. And although he was privy to the fact that I was not on birth control, he told all of our mutual friends that I had tried to trap him with a pregnancy. The entire situation left me broken hearted for a lot of years.

Several years had gone by before I married another man. I am a prophetic and lucid dreamer. It is extremely difficult for me to read for myself, so my angels and divine essence help to guide me in life through my dreaming experience. One of my favorite dream interpretation books is a book called *The Dreamer's Dictionary* that I have been using for years. It is a reference to anything and everything you could dream about and what it means. My angels know I use this book as a reference, so whenever I have a prophetic dream I know exactly how to interpret what the angels are trying to tell me in my dream messages. It draws the correlations between the dream and what the reader is experiencing in real life. It has helped me to predict things about my life that I otherwise would not have the capability of doing.

Many years later, I woke up one morning and recalled a lucid visitation from a young boy who came to me in a dream. When he appeared, the first words that came out of his mouth were "Mom, it's me." I couldn't fully grasp who this young man was in the dream until I had fully awoken. Even though he told me in the dream "mom its me"

He was wearing a red and white Ohio State sports jersey, was very tall like his father, and looked just like me in the face with long brown beach wave-style hair like mine. He was so sweet and so handsome. From what I could pick up from his essence, I believe that he would have been an athlete and someone who loved music and was very spiritually grounded, just like his mom. When I woke up, from this experience. The handsome young man recalled the miscarriage I had years prior to this experience the handsome young man in my dream turned out the be young man that came to visit me in my dreams was my son that I had miscarried. When I woke up I instantly did the math and when I had the dream he would have been about 18 years old. Upon meeting him on that level and having such a beautiful interaction with him, I decided to give him the name Brandon. I now have a permanent connection to him and it filled a very deep void inn my heart from losing a child.

Brandon is always with me. I feel his presence everywhere I go. I know he is one of my angels, watching over me and guiding me through life. I have seen his father a few times and he has never mentioned any experiences with the child although I have forgiven him and we remain a very distant friendship to this day and are always happy to see one another when we occasionally run into one another.

Testimonial

Lynn

"Susan picked up immediately without me even having to tell her about how my baby died in utero and how I had to go through the entire labor and delivery process knowing my baby wasn't alive. Susan assured me that it was not my fault, I had done everything right. She explained understandingly, that it was the most horrible day of her life. The soul of the child explained to me that its brain wasn't developing correctly and decided a life with those kinds of limitations was not something this particular soul did not want to go through because the child wanted to be an athlete. A few years later he came back to the same parents and was born in full health to complete his life mission! Thank you for helping me to understand Susan"

Racheal

I had been trying to conceive for a few months because my husband and I were ready to start a family. A few short weeks later a plus sign showed up on my pregnancy test and we were elated and told everyone immediately. A few short months later I began to experience heavy cramping and bleeding and ended up in the hospital having a miscarriage. Susan immediately picked up on my child and explained to me what had happened with the fetus not developing properly that is why the miscarriage happened. I had always though it was something that I had done wrong and Susan's message that day made my heart open wide and she also confirmed that my 2 year old son had reincarnated into my son that I have now who has a completely healthy body with no limitations. Thank you Susan I had no idea how deeply this had been effecting me and now I have peace in my heart.

CHAPTER VI

Comforting Spiritual Answers on Sudden Infant Death Syndrome SIDS

Sudden infant death syndrome (SIDS) occurs when a healthy baby under the age of one dies suddenly and unexpectedly. Healthcare professionals are unsure why SIDS happens. However, certain factors can put a baby at risk of SIDS. SIDS is the most common cause of death in infants less than 1 year of age in the United States.

Taking steps to reduce risk factors, such as following safe sleep recommendations for infants, may help prevent SIDS. When a healthy baby under the age of 1 dies, and a thorough clinical investigation is unable to find the cause of death, a doctor may diagnose SIDS. SIDS has no warning signs or visible symptoms.

I, personally, have never had to suffer through such a loss of having a baby in the later stages of pregnancy die in the womb and having to give birth to a deceased child or lost a child to SIDS. My condolences go out to anyone who has ever had to endure such a heartbreaking experience. I had my apprehensions as to whether or not to include a chapter on the subject matter as well, but having known so many women and their families that have endured this level of heartbreak who never had the chance to know their child, I felt like this was a necessary topic to include.

As a professional psychic medium, I view this topic much differently than the average person may perceive a situation such as this. From what I've learned about SIDS from the souls on the other side, that many of them come into our lives for such a short period of time for one reason.

That reason being the desire to experience something that we call "Unconditional Love" This was all their soul desired in order to complete their life lesson.

Some of the souls of the children who have passed away in utero, or shortly after birth, also tell me that sometimes there may have been problems in development, either physically or mentally. There are countless brave souls who make the decision to incarnate with disabilities. They exhibit traits of tremendous bravery and valor. For those souls who require full physical and mental capabilities to fulfill their life purpose, but have been put in the situation where they would live a life filled with struggle, they often choose to live life shortly after birth or in utero. The vast majority of the souls who make this arduous decision have informed me that there is nothing different that their parents could have done to save them.

Often times in these situations, the mothers who have lost their children had the opportunity to hold them after the child took their last breath. I cannot imagine such pain and suffering that accompanies this nightmare and my heart and soul goes out to the parents.

In the vast majority of such an occurrence, the child will incarnate back into the same family. Several years ago, a family member of mine had lost a baby shortly after the birth. Although I had not seen a picture of this child, I did tell my relative that the baby would be back within a year and a half. Because the mother was able to see and hold the child that died shortly after birth, the mother knew the appearance of her baby son that was born and died.

A year and a half later, I had given my relative a reading that she let me know that she was expecting another baby and was thrilled . This new baby boy when he was born was a spitting image of the one who had passed away prematurely. I was convinced that this was the same soul, but immediately reincarnated into a different body so that he would have all the necessary abilities to carry out his life's purpose without any obstructions to stand in his way. When I spoke with the mother after the birth, she confirmed this was indeed the same child. Once he was born and she was able to gaze into his eyes, she knew they were the same eyes as her baby that had passed away previously.

I want to make it clear that in these situations, there wasn't anything the parents did wrong, or could have done, to save their child's life. I have done so many readings for many people who have endured such a hardship and continue to carry on the guilt of their child's death. For anyone who has experienced such an unfortunate experience such as this, please be aware that the child will come back to you; either as a child of your own, or reincarnated into your same family or close friends so the mother and/or father can still be an active part of their lives.

Testimonial

Darla

"Many years ago my baby girl passed away 3 days after birth due to sudden infant death syndrome. Susan had no way of knowing that this had happened in my life. Susan described her crib, her bedroom, her blankets and even the colors on the wall. Susan, let me know that the baby had an undetected heart defect that was actually confirmed, as the reason for this child's passing. For many years, Even though the doctors told us it was a heart defect I could not accept that fact that I was asleep and had no idea that my baby had stopped breathing. This put me into the deepest depression a person can even begin to experience. I thought that my baby died because I was sleeping and had not been right there with her when she wasn't breathing. Susan discussed with me at great length the personality of my child how much she loved me what she looked like which was exact. I finally after all of these years have peace in my heart and access to my daughter soul at anytime."

CHAPTER VII

"I wish I weren't here sometimes" My husband, my stepson & the broken foster care and Children Services system

Anyone who has ever dealt with the Foster Care System and Children's Services knows that these people who work for these establishments are way overworked and underpaid and have deep gratitude for their selfless choice of profession. Thank you for all of the caring humanitarians that try their best to help children, families and support legal action when necessary problems occur. The amount of children whose parents are unable to take care of them is growing in numbers partly due to the ongoing drug crisis going on globally and will continue to be an even larger problem as humanity moves forward.

I met my husband Alexander on a crisp November day. My husband is a very quiet man, quite the opposite of myself. He has a beautiful soul, a heart without limitations and wonderful intentions for all of humanity. What he lacks for in words, he makes up for in compassion.

During a recent conversation between the two of us, he blurted out the words "'I wish I would've never been born. I wish my mother would've aborted me. The emotional toll it put me through as a child, there were so many days that I would wish that I never had to come to this Earth and can deeply relate to the feelings of how the un aborted are experiencing. In all honesty growing up at the hands of my mother figure as a young person I remember feeling the same way when things would go to a point of spirit breaking."

We are survivors, not victims, we both turned out to be great hearted people and now are so happy that we ARE here. My husband Alexander was given up for adoption as a young child and wound up under the care of his grandparents. He had a twin sister and one older brother that stayed with the biological parents. However, shortly after his grandparents took custody, they were deemed as too old to serve as his guardians. He was then transferred into foster care.

"You bring this life into the world," Alexander began to tell me. "And then you don't take any responsibility for it and then you expect it to grow up and be normal when it's always wondering where it came from and where it belongs." That's cruelty was his opinion, directing that at his biological parents. "As humans, we're supposed to be together," he stated."If you can't control your child, then I'm sorry, but you should've never had the child to begin with. And now the child will always feel unwanted in the world. You wonder why there's so much depravity now is because some parents don't bother to take care of their own."

He remembers at the age of three, being beaten so bad with a belt by his father he had to be taken to his grandparents home for safety. After that, he never saw anyone in his biological family again. He had a twin sister and a brother that continued to live on with the biological family. Because of the circumstances surrounding his departure from his biological family, he never understood why he was given away and the other siblings got to stay. I completely understand, why he feels this way. Not all adopted children share the about their situation and are very happy with the families they were adopted into wonderful families were they were better off.

Aside from having to fight for his own food and endure extreme child abuse that continued in foster care, it caused him to lose all sense of identity. He spent so much time trying to fit in, which was an impossible task considering he didn't know who he was or where he came from.

After a year and a half of being in the foster care program, Alexander was coming upon his fourth year of life. Back in the day, if the child had not yet been adopted by age four, they would go into the system permanently. My husband was truly blessed that his adoptive parents found him right before his fourth birthday. During that time, the cut-off age for adopting a child was 40 years old and his adoptive parents almost hit that mark.

My husband had an instant connection with his beautiful adoptive mother. Although his adoptive father loved him, they had a challenging relationship at times. But they took Alexander in and raised him as their own. I do believe that adoptive parents love their children as their own. The majority of people I know that have been adopted have had wonderful experiences with their adoptive families.

Although my husband was brought into a family with a mother that adored him dearly and raised him as her own, there came an awful day when the truth came running out of his father's mouth during a heated discussion that broke my husband's spirit permanently. My husband and his first wife were having trouble conceiving and were considering adoption. So, Alexander went to his father for advice. His father looked at him and said "You will never love an adopted child as much as you would love a child of your own."

From early childhood memories, Alexander knew that he was a biological twin. He has a twin sister and a biological older brother, whom his biological parents would never allow him to see due to circumstances beyond his control. He believes he was put up for adoption because his parents wanted the American dream of a family consisting of one boy and one girl. He wound up being the second boy. He believes it was easier for his family to get rid of him and keep going without him so they could convey that image of perfection.

"I understand that sometimes trauma opens up places that people don't want to go," Alexander said. "Trauma is an incident that teaches us something profound. No matter what, as long as you're still breathing, that experience taught you something. If you can't learn from that experience, whether spiritually, physically or mentally, then that trauma wasn't big enough to impact you."

CHAPTER VIII

Dr John The Episcopalian "Church of the Un-aborted"

Directly before this book was supposed to go into editing, I felt it absolutely necessary to include an experience from my Chiropractor, Dr. John P. While Dr John was adjusting me, I told him about this book that you are reading now. He immediately shared with me a very interesting experience that he had downtown during the middle of a day when he went into visit a church that was open. My sweet chiropractor, who is also a dear friend whom I consider to be extended family, inquired as to the personal happenings occurring in my life. I proceeded to tell him about this book I had decided to write last minute, due to what was currently occurring in the world and had put my other book on hold.

When I went on to explain to him that I was composing a book on a psychic- medium's perspective on abortion, he lit up like an overly lit Christmas tree.

"I have a story that is going to blow your mind," John exclaimed, his voice trembling out of excitement.

John is an incredibly friendly man that could strike up a conversation with just about anyone. He has an affinity for old churches and a fascination with old architecture and varying world religions. He was wandering through downtown Columbus one day when he suddenly stopped in front of a church on a Wednesday afternoon. The parking lot was filled to the brim during a time when churches are fighting for their congregations and most churches are closing their doors annually by 20% in the United States.

John proceeded to make his way inside and sat down among a significant amount of people. He was perplexed that there was no actual, traditional service taking place. He began to ask the strangers seated beside him if there was going to be a service. After they responded with a resounding "no," he asked why if the church was so full, why was it lacking a service.

Many people proceeded to join in on the conversation to inform my friend why there would be no formal service. They gathered around John to express that they were all children who were forced into this world because the Catholic Church had chastised their parents into believing abortion was wrong. These were the unwanted children whose parents did not abort them. Once the children were born, they received little to no care, essentially left to raise themselves while predominantly in and out of foster care, abusive juvenile detention centers because they were homeless, starving and uneducated.

Due to the fact that most of these people were homeless, the pastor of the church left the church open all day, every day, so that they would have a place to come and stay if they needed warmth, shelter, or any kind of spiritual guidance. These were abandoned children who had no one to care for them.

The vast majority of these children John got to know were completely abandoned as children. After speaking with these lost souls, John approached the priest to interview her. The priest went on to explain to him that, due to the departed Queen of England, there has been a long history of women in power and made way for more women taking a leadership role in the church. The pastor of this specific church went on to explain that the Catholic church and other denominations primarily only care about the souls before they are born. I believe that she was referring to those in religious power rather than the general congregations. I especially believe this because this book is being written because my old office happened to be right next to a room where the people from the congregation involved with were caring enough to pray for the souls of the aborted children.

I recall several years ago, I came across a quote from a priest stating "If you can get a child before seven years of age, you will have them for life. Meaning early life programming with religion and dogma because children are so impressionable, the churches until the age of seven means that the church believes they have gotten into the subconscious minds of the children, so they will be giving money to the church for the rest of their lives."

John went on and expressed to me that he himself had been raised in the Catholic Church. He said he was surrounded by a bunch of beer drinking, hard-working Catholics. He expressed his frustration regarding how the churches never had really taught about our spiritual gifts. I 110% agree with him. He even went on to ask the minister what they would do with a child such as Jesus, if his mother had wanted to abort him.

I want to make it clear that although it appears as though I'm targeting the Catholic Church and some of its beliefs, I still have much admiration for Catholicism and world religions of all kinds. I believe there are beneficial aspects toward religion other than negative connotations. I was raised in a Christian/Lutheran church. My faith and my upbringing gave me a foundation to question so that later in life I could do research and form my own opinions about what felt right to me.

Regardless of my beliefs, or those of others, please feel free to form your own beliefs. We all have free will and the beauty of that is getting to embrace who we are what we believe in.

CHAPTER IX

Plants and Herbs used culturally throughout history to prevent Pregnancy

This chapter XI is a historical compilation of plants, roots and seeds that were once used to prevent pregnancy and is not intended to be any sort of medical advice.

Always consult your Medical Doctor as some plants can be poisonous or cause allergies.

No form of birth control is 100% fool-proof. Therefore, in my personal opinion, abstinence Is a woman's only guarantee to never conceive. However, I am keenly aware that for the vast majority of the population, abstinence isn't an option. Human beings are of a sexual nature; it's ingrained in us and is dominant in our biological makeup. We need not be ashamed of such sexual desires and sensations, however precautions do need to be taken when trying to avoid pregnancy.

Birth control for men will be a part of the medical future, sooner rather than later. Although this advancement will not entirely solve the issue of unwanted pregnancy, it has come to my attention that men are thinking twice about being sexually irresponsible and fathering several children. In this modern era, both men and women are being held accountable for the financial responsibilities of parenting and possibly now facing being responsible in the future for home schooling their children if school shooting continues, which they have increased. Thank God for every Child Support Enforcement Agency and for the laws that have been passed to hold parents legally accountable for paying the expenses that it takes to raise a child.

Due to the implementation of this impending ban, I would highly recommend that women start gathering seeds and harvesting their own herbal remedies, only to be consumed under medical doctor supervision if there comes a day that we may be in a situation when a person does not have access to medical birth control.

Based on today's state of affairs, it appears as though we may in fact be entering into the Dark Ages. If abortion is indeed outlawed in its entirety, women will have no choice but to go to unauthorized, dangerous sources, or partake in what was formerly referred to as coat hanger abortions.

When unwanted children were conceived, many women were forced to subject themselves to not only unsavory conditions, but to unsanitary objects used to illegally abort a fetus. Many women have died as a result of punctures to their uterus, often times resulting in fatal bleeding. There is also the harsh reality that an illicit abortion may not always successfully eliminate the pregnancy, resulting in a significant chance to birth defects to the baby. I just watched a Dr. Phil show with two daughters of a drug addicted mother and the mothers attempt to terminate her pregnancy left this beautiful young daughter with a lot of disabilities. Among other physical health risks that accompany illegal abortions are failure to remove or expel all pregnancy tissue from the uterus, in addition to hemorrhaging, infection and damage to the genital tract and internal organs as a consequence of inserting dangerous objects into the vagina.

Another grave concern accompanying the Roe v. Wade overturn are the laws stating that if a woman is raped or her life is in danger because of the pregnancy that she would be allowed to legally obtain an abortion. While this is obviously beneficial for actual rape victims and women whose lives are at risk, this may play host to a completely new set of problems. Another possibility could be men who played an innocent part in a pregnancy and had consensual intercourse to be accused of rape simply on the basis that the mother wanted an abortion.

CHAPTER X

Natural Birth Control - not a for sure guarantee, but has been used for centuries in other cultures for pregnancy prevention. This is not medical advice always consult with your medical doctor.

Is it possible that birth control pills, diaphragms, spermicides, IUD's, morning after pill, the birth control shots could someday be considered as devices that cause abortions?? Is that what we all MAY be facing? If people in power have the ability to outlaw abortion in some states please keep in mind that these same people could decide to outlaw birth control. I have listed some plants that may possibly be helpful and safe to use for birth control.

For this chapter I must recommend that the readers get a really good book, website or knowledge base on what is called Foraging. Foraging is learning how to identify wild plants that grow in nature that are edible, free and delicious. Because there is herbal information and plant information in this book, I would highly recommend the practice of learning foraging to anyone! Most people do not have any idea that you can go right out in your backyard and eat for free as long as it is not chemically treated!

Another tradition you might want to learn about is Ayurvedic, the traditional Hindu system of Medicine. I was able to find a lot of information on plants, herbs, roots and several recommendations for naturally preventing pregnancy. Ayurvedic is an ancient beautiful tradition that is rooted in Hindu Culture. From what I have experienced with using Ayurvedic along with Western Medicine the two compliment one another very well. Always ask your medical doctor if this type of practice if they believe this approach would have a positive effect on your well being,

We can eat for free in certain areas year round if you live in the correct climate. By having this knowledge, we can live that way as long as there is a clean water supply, without having to run to the grocery store every five minutes.

Because a lot of plants look similar, there are also applications that can be downloaded on your cell phones that will identify every plant that you take a picture of and tell you if it is poisonous, people friendly, edible, the medicinal qualities of the plant and some of them will even tell you what the plant will taste like. I had no idea that people can eat cat tails until I started learning the art of foraging. Apparently there is an edible pulp inside of the cat tail that is very nutritious and delicious. Although this is the book of a completely different nature, I had to add the importance in about learning foraging and what plants could possibly be harmful or medicinal. Once again please consult your doctor.

Queen Anns Lace

While preparing to write this book, I went on an educational journey to find holistic approaches toward preventing pregnancy. During an enlightened conversation with a spiritual advisor of mine, they made mention of Queen Anne's Lace, an abundant weed so common in many areas of the United States that can even be found in residential lawns. However, as plentiful as an herb it may be, there are signs of it becoming outlawed based on its effects to deter reproduction.

Due to the implementation of this impending law, I would highly recommend that people start gathering seeds and harvesting their own herbal remedies, under doctor supervision of course. Another recommendation is getting a book on Foraging.

I would recommend everyone learn how to forage and learn how to survive off of the land. I even learned from my foraging book that all in all, cattails may be the perfect survival food as long as it is picked in an area that doesn't have chemically treated water. Although I don't have cattail plants listed in this book as a possible means of preventing pregnancy, I thought it would be a great example to use in this book and not many people I know have a clue about foraging and living off the land. I highly recommend knowing as much as you can about this topic. *Gardening know How: Cattails in the Kitchen

Another easier way to identify plants are through cell phone applications that are made to specifically identify what plant you have taken a picture of the plant. Once the picture of the plant is taken the application will identify the plant for you and give you all information you need to know about the properties, safety information and uses .

Aside from Queen's Lace, there are several naturally alternate ways of actually preventing pregnancy. While these methods are not foolproof, several of them have been scientifically proven to be helpful toward the determent of conception.

Ingesting such foods as papaya, pineapple, apricot, ginger, dried figs, cinnamon, asafetida, parsley, Neem and vitamin C supplements directly after intercourse have shown promising signs of helping fertility and pregnancy.

LITHOSPERMUM RUDER

Many Native American tribes utilized the herbal properties of the Wild Stoneseed root, it's formal name is Lithospermum Ruder. Mixed in either a cold drink or ingested via smoking, the roots

purpose is to enact permanent sterilization. The Native Americans that implemented this method would consume it daily for a period of six months before sterilization would go into effect.

Although there haven't been any recent studies done on the Wild Stoneseed Root, in 1945, the U.S. Department of Agriculture, through pharmaceutical research, confirmed that the plant could be properly adapted as a method of birth control. Although no studies have been conducted on humans since the USDA study in 1945, additional studies have been performed on animals since, all which yielded positive results.

MILK THISTLE

In addition to the Stoneseed root, Native Americans also used milk thistle as a means to **decrease** fertility. Milk thistle was brought to Native Americans by European settlers, adopted thereafter by various tribes. In addition to infertility, milk thistle has also been used for additional purposes, such as restoring liver and kidney damage.

There is a lack of recent research to confirm whether milk thistle is an effective form of contraceptive, but if this has piqued your interest, I would suggest seeking out testimonials online or consulting your doctor to determine for yourself if this is a viable option.

WILD CARROT SEED

In specific regions of India, wild carrot seed is directed to be ingested immediately after intercourse to prevent conception. Following the initial dose of wild carrot seed directly after sex, it is required to consume one tea spoon daily for the duration of the following week in order to render its effectiveness.

A recent study has been conducted on the history and efficiency of the wild carrot seed as an approach to birth control. While the capability of the contraceptive results reign true, the reasoning behind its successful performance still remains unknown. However, further research is continuing.

GINGER PICTURE

Those who subscribe to the natural healing methods say that drinking one quart of ginger tea daily for up to five days can force menstruation. Alternatively, you can also combine a teaspoon of ginger with six ounces of boiling water to achieve the same effects as ginger tea. Women who have a confirmed pregnancy are recommended to avoid ginger due to its ability to lead to miscarriage. Ginger has many beneficial health properties as well as preventing pregnancy.

APRICOT KERNAL

If you're tracking your menstrual cycle and are aware that you'll be ovulating in the near future, apricot kernels can be used as an applicable birth control method. They have the power to reduce the chances of fertilization immediately after ovulation.

Apricot kernels require a keen sense of timing when used for the intended purposes. Consuming apricot kernels immediately before intercourse or immediately prior to ovulation will not provide the desired results.

RUE HERB

Rue herb teas have demonstrated to prevent implementation of sperm by decreasing the capillary permeability in the uterus. In order to successfully keep sperm from reaching their intended destination, boil a cup of water and two tablespoons of rue tea. Allow the mixture to steep for five minutes to release necessary compounds. Consume the tea two to three times a day in the event of an unplanned pregnancy to induce abortion effects.

Take note that if three teaspoons are ingested at one time, there is a stronger risk of kidney complications and negative effects of the nervous system.

BUCKWHEAT HERB

Similar to the intended results of rue herb, buckwheat herbs have the same properties that contribute toward preventing implementation of the sperm. After the initial consumption, the herb produces an adrenaline effect, causing the uterus to deplete the essential nutrients to an already fertilized egg. For best results, the substance should be consumed before and after intercourse.

The most beneficial feature of the buckwheat herb is that there are no known side effects, aside from the fact that it should be avoided before any major surgeries.

Buckwheat can be found in many common staples such as oatmeal, various pastas, breads, pastries, vinegar, and a multitude of other foods.

ASCORBIC ACID VITAMIN C

Vitamin C, a vitamin so common that it is consumed by hundreds of millions of humans a day, does in fact have contraceptive properties. Vitamin C is packed full of ascorbic acid, which can decrease the prominence of progesterone whose most fundamental importance is to preserve pregnancy.

There are notable risk factors involved in consuming too much vitamin C. Some medical professional advice yields against using vitamin C tablets for contraception. It's always a sensible idea to stay well-informed and receive a second opinion from a doctor or gynecologist before implementing vitamin c into a regular birth control regimen.

While there are additional ways of preventing pregnancies, such as the rhythm method, nothing is fool proof. I am not a doctor offering any form of medical advice.

CHAPTER XI

Necessary Information To Consider

Roe V. Wade came with its fair share of controversy. It was also accompanied by an abundance of rhetoric and falsifications regarding abortion that bore little to no truth. Some deceitful accusations that have been sprouted state that abortion has the potential to lead to blindness, depression, breast cancer and a plethora of other health issues. These claims are not only erroneous allegations, but have no factual backing to these claims.

What is a credible proclamation is that during the time when abortions were illegal, they were regarded as highly dangerous and incredibly life threatening. Those that sought out abortions prior to when Roe V Wade was enacted were exposed to a multitude of health complications, both during and following the procedure.

Abortion had initially been a moderately accepted practice in America following the founding of this country. The state of Connecticut became the first state to outlaw abortions and prohibited any use of poisons or herbs to terminate a pregnancy. New York followed suit in 1929, establishing later term abortions as a felony and those performed in earlier trimesters as a misdemeanor.

Following New York's new set of guidelines regarding abortion, ten more states rendered similar protocol regarding abortion by the late 1870s. These initial regulations had strict repercussions not only for the performing doctor, but for the women who requested their services. These legal protocols were established to "protect the women." However, by the late 1850s, abortion was still not considered a crime in 21 states. This began to change in the 1860s. In 1882, West Virginia implemented a code that criminalized abortion, enacting a ten year prison sentence for both doctor and patient.

Back alley abortions, performed by unlicensed doctors, were predominantly executed by use of a coat hanger or other blunt objects used to pierce the uterus. On other occasions, herbal remedies were provided with the intent of discontinuing the pregnancy.

Studies show that five to ten thousand American women met their untimely demise each year prior to Roe V Wade due to these adverse methods of procuring abortions on their own. The most common cause of death was hemorrhaging or infection.

On average, 40 million abortions are performed both legally and illegally around the globe, while 19 million back alley abortions continue to be carried out yearly in developing countries. The average age for the recipient of an abortion ranges between 15 and 24 years of age.

Over the past 30 years, hundreds of abortion clinics have been bombed by anti- abortionist groups, killing and injuring an average of 69,000 people.

While the decision to overturn Roe v Wade is implementing harsh restrictions on women's rights to choose, it has not yet been deemed outright illegal by all 50 states. While 26 states have banned the practice, it is left up to the remaining 24 to implement their own laws in regard to this matter. The overturn transferred the ruling control over to state governments, most of which have already eluded to the idea that terminating a pregnancy will be deemed illegal.

Following the initial overturn in 2022, Missouri became the first state in the country to immediately ban any termination of pregnancy. Kentucky, Louisiana and South Dakota quickly followed suit. However, exceptions can be made if a woman's life is in danger and is declared a medical emergency.

In any other circumstance that doesn't involve a life-threatening danger, anyone who provides or receives an abortion will not only be charged with a felony, but can face fines up to $100,000 given the state the procedure is performed.

In Idaho, Tennessee and Texas, abortions after six weeks had already been declared illegal before the overturn while West Virginia's only abortion clinic closed its doors immediately following the overturn.

The state of Alabama put an abortion ban into effect in 2019, while in the same year, Attorney General Dave Yost of Ohio passed a law that prohibited abortions around six weeks, or alternatively when the fetus's heartbeat could be detected.

Another dire concern that I have regarding this law going into affect is due to the safety of the rights of men in the United States. Some of these laws state that women are able to get an abortion if they have been raped. It concerns me deeply that some women may be so desperate in their situation that they could emotionally unstable and accused innocent men of rape!

This is a very serious concern that I have as a psychic, medium! I have already seen some of these things happening in my psychic visions. The only advice that I can offer to men in a situation such as this is to try and prevent this from happening is abstinence, and we all know more than likely that will not happen!.

Please just be sure that you know someone that you were being intimate with on a deep level. Unfortunately, through the course of my years of being a Professional Psychic Medium, I have seen way too many men get trapped into pregnancies, because the women misled the man by believing that a woman is on birth control. I have predicted many of these situations very accurately, when it comes to women being manipulative about wanting to have a children. Of course not all women are manipulative to this degree however, we are living in a world today where talk show drama is very played upon and young people are influenced by the craziness going on on these platforms and are follow suit.

CHAPTER XII

World and Cultural Belief on Abortion

In Ancient Greece, abortion was a rather controversial topic within the culture, with varying viewpoints. Philosophers, medical professionals, lawyers, scholars, historians and even poets took on their own individual perspectives regarding the subject at hand. The general public engaged in disparate viewpoints, much like those in today's political climate.

The issue of abortion tended to be monetarily motivated in certain circumstances, the parental units wanting to avoid financial burdens that accompanied raising a child. Others wanted to avoid the procreation of children that could be perceived as weak and inept.

Those who opposed the practice usually did so on behalf of the father of the unborn. Although abortion wasn't necessarily opposed to by the Greeks or the Romans, the paternal figures of the unborn child would often times contest the practice of abortion. This was mainly due to the entitlement they felt when it came to the possession of the child. Women would often times face condemnation and even death for their actions.

In Ancient Greece and Rome, it was often theorized that the fetus didn't form any semblance of humanity until 40 days if the unborn were male and 80 days if it were female. Aristotle came upon this conclusion from his observation on children who had been the subject of miscarriages.

Hippocrates (400-357 B.C.) was a renowned physician in Ancient Greece, deemed to be the father of modern medicine. Medical professionals to this day implement his studies into their daily practice. Hippocrates even began his own school for medicine around 400 B.C. on the island of Kos, where a significant amount of his philosophies were conceived. Hippocrates is also responsible for the renowned The Oath of Hippocrates, most commonly referred to at the Hippocratic Oath, currently upheld by modern day medical professionals.

In the Oath Of Hippocrates, he stated "I swear by Apollo the physician, and Aesculapius the surgeon, likewise Hygeia and Panacea, and call all the gods and goddesses to witness, that I will observe and keep this underwritten oath, to the utmost of my power and judgment. I will reverence my master who taught me the art. Equally with my parents, will I allow him things necessary for his support, and will consider his sons as brothers. I will teach them my art without reward or agreement; and I will impart all my acquirement, instructions, and whatever I know, to my master's children, as to my own; and likewise to all my pupils, who shall bind and tie themselves by a professional oath, but to none else. With regard to healing the sick, I will devise and order for them the best diet, according to my judgment and means; and I will take care that they suffer no hurt or damage. Nor shall any man's entreaty prevail upon me to administer poison to anyone; neither will I counsel any man to do so. Moreover, I will give no sort of medicine to any pregnant woman, with a view to destroy the child."

Hippocrates' philosophies have been a presence in such cases as Roe v. Wade and is often associated with various pro-life arguments. His ideologies have fortified more pro-life stances on abortion and has reinforced right-wing doctrines.

The Hippocratic Oath wasn't translated until the 1700s when Western medical professionals implemented it into their practice. The World Medical Association in Geneva officially acquired in 1948 and was rewritten in 1964 by the Dean of Tufts University School of Medicine by Louis Lasagna. In this revised version, there is no restriction on abortion.

Aristotle

Aristotle was a prolific philosopher, with one of his major contributions establishing the Lyceum, an acclaimed school in Athens. It's difficult to properly determine his most valued intellectual bestowment upon society, both historically and carried into the modern world, but his scientific method made a critical impact on society as we know it. This encompassed areas of chemistry, psychology, politics, biology, botany and logic. He is also responsible for the theory of relativity which states "everything was made of matter, shape, substance, and structure and the changes in them were the results of the organism trying to reach its potential."

Aristotle identified an analytical contrast among what is a simple fetus and a living, breathing soul. He condoned fetal termination based on its inability to possess the same senses that humans retain. He viewed fetuses simply as that; a fetus. He recognized them as lifeless beings with the inefficiency to possess a human soul.

In book VII of the Politics, Aristotle transcribed "as to exposing or rearing the children born, let there be a law that no deformed child shall be reared; but on the ground of number of children, if the regular customs hinder any of those born being exposed, there must be a limit fixed to the procreation of offspring, and if any people have a child as a result of intercourse in contrvantion of these regulations, abortion must be practiced on it before it has developed sensation and life; for the line between lawful and unlawful abortion will be marked by the fact of having sensation and being alive."

PLATO

Plato was a philosopher in Athens, thought to be one of the most influential figures in Western Philosophy and coined the term Platonism. He studied directly under Aristotle and was a mentor to Aristole. He was also known to be a direct impactor of religion upon society. He established the Platonist school of thought, which was the first academy of educational learning in Europe.

Plato was also known to be a direct impactor of religion upon society. The most formative contribution to society at the time was the Forms, which is the genesis of Platonism.

The Forms…In the Republic, composed in 461 B.C., Plato stated ""When the men and women get past the age for procreation,…we'll release them and allow them the freedom to have sex with anyone they want…But before we release them, we'll impress upon them the importance of trying their best to abort absolutely every pregnancy that occurs, and of ensuring that any baby born despite their efforts is not brought up."

His proclamation goes along with that of Aristotle's in Politics; ""Where there are too many (for in our state population has a limit), when couples have children in excess, and the state of feeling is averse to the exposure of offspring, let abortion be procured before sense and life have begun ; what may or may not be lawfully done in these cases depends on the question of life and sensation"

CHAPTER XIII

World View And Facts

The United States isn't the only country to have taken a stance against abortions. Throughout the world, each country has implemented its own laws regarding pregnancy termination.

The annual average of abortions performed globally is approximately 73 million, according to the World Health Organization. In countries with legalized abortion, nearly 90 percent of them are safe. In countries where abortion is prohibited, that number significantly drops down to 25 percent.

24 countries around the globe have restricted abortion in its entirety. Approximately 100 countries have regulations in place, most of which limit who can and cannot receive abortions.

Prior to the overturn of Roe v. Wade, 97% of unsafe abortions were performed in developing countries, half of which occur in Asia, predominately central and south Asia. In Africa and Latin America, an approximated 75% of abortions are considered risky, while around half of all procedures in Africa fall under the same umbrella.

In 1994, the United Nations organized the Internal Conference on Population and Development (ICPD). This took place in Cairo, Egypt from September 5 through the 13th of that same year. 20,000 members from governments across the globe were in attendance alongside various UN organizations and the members of the media. Several nongovernmental organizations were present as well.

Unsafe abortion practices were a topic of discussion, as well as family planning, birth control, infant death rates, women's education and immigration.

While American policy has put more of a restraint on abortion, several other countries around the world have changed their stance since 2020. Mexico decriminalized pregnancy termination, while Argentina and Thailand legalized the practice. Below are the abortion policies enacted by various countries around the world.

AFRICA

The continent of Africa houses 54 individual countries. Out of those 54 countries, only ten have lenient abortion rights. Also home to the African continent is The Protocol to the African Charter on Human and People's Rights of Women in Africa, more commonly known as the Maputo Protocol. This protocol, implemented in 2003 by the African Union not only promotes access to reproductive rights, but serves as an advocate for equal rights for women on both a social and political scale. The charter has also fought for an end to genital mutilation, which has been a fairly common practice used for centuries.

BOSTWANA

Women in Botswana are granted the most accessible abortions in Sub-Saharan Africa, but not without its restrictions. There is a 16 week limit and all abortions must be conducted in a government hospital and approved by two doctors. Because of these restrictions, unsafe abortion practices are still being sought out by women throughout the country, a significant amount resulting in the death of the mother.

There's a custom in Botswana called lobolo. This is a tradition where a woman's family is monetarily compensated by the man to marry her. The men, having essentially paid for their bride, have the pre-conceived notion that they are the rightful owner's of their wife's body. This infringes on the woman's reproductive rights. So although women are entitled in Botswana to an abortion up to 16 weeks based on certain circumstances, the husband ultimately has the final say.

CENTRAL AFRICA REPUBLICA

Abortion in the Central African Republic is restricted nearly in its entirety. The only exception being as a result of rape, as rape and sexual assault was rather commonplace in this territory. Any entity that executes an abortion is subjected for up to five years in prison, in addition to a fine. Any physician partaking in such a procedure is at risk of losing their medical license for five years.

Prior to 2006, pregnancy termination in Chad was deemed an illegal practice. That same year, the National Assembly of Chad decriminalized the practice, permitting it strictly in the cases of sexual assault and incest.

EGYPT

Cameroon's abortion laws follow that of much of the countries residing in the African continent. They are severely restrictive, permitting exceptions exclusively for those with at-risk pregnancy conditions, mental health, rape or incest. Those seeking abortions outside these risks are exposed to unsafe practices that could be life threatening.

Egypt implemented the Penal Code of 1937. Articles 260-264 outlaws abortion. Under Article 61, however, of the same code, exclusions may apply during life threatening conditions for the mother.

In any other case, absolutely no exemption will be taken into consideration. Those that do undergo an abortion procedure face a prison sentence anywhere from six months to three years, stated in article 262 of the Penal Code. A doctor who performs the operation can face a punishment of three to 15 years.

KENYA

Under the Constitution of Kenya (2010), Article 26 (4). Right to Life states:
"Abortion is not permitted unless, in the opinion of a trained health professional, there is need for emergency treatment, or the life or health of the mother is in danger, or if permitted by any other written law."
Under the Penal Code, Laws of Kenya, Cap. 63, Revised Edition 2009 (20080, Articles 158-160, 228 and 240 states the following:

Article 158. Attempts of procure abortion.
"Any person who, with intent to procure miscarriage of a woman, whether she is or is not with child, unlawfully administers to her or causes her to take any poison or other noxious thing, or uses any force of any kind, or uses any other means whatever, is guilty of a felon and is liable ti imprisonment for fourteen years."

Article 160. Supplying drugs or instruments to procure abortion.
"Any person who unlawfully supplies to or procures for any person any thing whatever, knowing that it is intended to be unlawfully used to procure miscarriage of a woman whether she is or is not with child, is guilty of a felony and is liable to imprisonment for three years."
Article 228. Killing unborn child

"Any person who, when a woman is about to be delivered of a child, prevents the child from being born alive by any act or omission of such a nature that, if the child had been born alive and had then died, he would be deemed to have unlawfully killed the child, is guilty of a felony and is liable to imprisonment for life." Somalia

Approximately 834,000 pregnancies occurred annually in Somalia between 2015-2019.

324,000 of those were unplanned, leaving 93,200 resulting in pregnancy termination. Abortion is legally accepted by the Somalian government only in the cases where a mother is facing life threatning conditions. Although, much like the United States, these practices are victim of a religious undertow brought forth by religious conservatism.

Due to the skyrocketing rate of maternal deaths due to unsafe abortion practices, post abortion care was established in Puntland, Somalia by Save the Children International. Not only does this organization focus on family planning following an abortion, but provides counseling, supplies and community partnership. 98% of PAC participants took advantage of the counseling, and out of those individuals, 88% went on a form of contraception.

AUSTRALIA

Abortion in Australia is legal in all states and territories. However, each state and territory are responsible for curating their own policies.

- Australian Capital Territory (ACT): A medical professional, whether it be a doctor or a nurse, can perform an abortion up to 16 weeks.
- New South Wales: A doctor can carry out a pregnancy termination up to 24 weeks of pregnancy. An abortion can be executed after 24 weeks if approved by two doctors.
- Northern Territory: 14 weeks is the limit if approved by one doctor. Two doctors must authorize any abortion between 14 and 23 weeks. Any procedure done after 23 weeks can only be approved under life threatening conditions.
- Queensland: Abortions are permitted up to 22 weeks after conception. Two doctors must approve any operation after 22 weeks.
- Northern Territory: 14 weeks is the limit if approved by one doctor. Two doctors must authorize any abortion between 14 and 23 weeks. Any procedure after 23 weeks can only be approved under life threatening conditions.
- South Australia: The cut off to receive an abortion is 22 weeks and six days. If the mother's life is at risk, or in the case of a multiple pregnancy where one fetus is severely impacting the life of another, then an abortion can be performed under the approval of two doctors. The same conditions apply if the fetus faces severe deformities.
- Tasmania: In the same case as ACT, an abortion is permissible until 16 weeks. Any procedure after that time must be approved by a doctor.
- Victoria: 24 weeks is the cut-off mark. However, after 24 weeks, two doctors can approve an abortion.
- Western Australia: Authorization is required by two doctors for an abortion up to 20 weeks. After 20 weeks, a government delegated council is required to authorize a termination of pregnancy.

Australia became the first territory to decriminalize abortion in 1998. Southern Australia was the most recent to do so in 2022.

The Offences Against the Person Act 1861 produced new laws that made abortion illegal in its entirety. Up until 1969, these laws were solidified, giving little to no leeway in regard to the law. The Menhennitt ruling in 1969, which was widely accepted in New South Wales and Queensland, legitimized abortion under the terms "if necessary to preserve the physical or mental health of the woman concerned, provided that the danger involved if the abortion did not outweigh the danger which the abortion was designed to prevent."

The Australian Labor Party introduced country-wide abortion legislation in 2019, stating that hospitals were mandated to performed abortions. This forced South Wales to decriminalize abortions. Abortions in New South Wales are available on request and partially covered by Medicare.

Northern Territory

The Termination of Pregnancy Law Reform Legislation Amendment Act 2021 was passed by the Legislative Assembly of Northern Territory on November 30, 2021.

It replaces the Termination of Pregnancy Act 2017, whose primary incentive was to expand the means for safe abortion. Under this legislation, a medical professional can carry out a pregnancy termination with the caviot that the woman is no more than 14 weeks pregnant. If a woman is between 14-23 weeks, the woman must obtain approval by two doctors.

The 2021 Act removes the need for assessment by a second doctor for terminations up to 24 weeks; "increases the gestational upper limit from 23 to 24 weeks"; and "allows terminations after 24 weeks gestation following consultation between two medical practitioners." It also "removes additional credentialing requirements for medical practitioners who perform termination of pregnancy over their existing credentialing" and "makes a consequential amendment to the Criminal Code."

The regulation "will benefit women in regional and remote communities who often travel hundreds, if not thousands, of kilometres for medical treatment." The Northern Territory health minister explained that 1% of abortions in the territory occur after 20 weeks, when serious or lethal anomaly was found. She said "[t]his highlights the incredibly small number of terminations that occur in the later stages, they are rare, complex situations," and "[i]t is a difficult debate for some people and can cause discomfort. I cannot overemphasize the importance of this for Territory women." Furthermore, in terms of allowing access to abortions after 24 weeks, she stated: "There is very little difference how a doctor clinically handles discovering a fetal anomaly at 20 weeks to one found at 30 weeks. What is different is that we do not currently have the framework to allow these clinical professionals to do their jobs."

NEW SOUTH WALES

On October 2, 2019, abortion was decriminalized in New South Wales due to the Abortion, Law Reform Act 2019. Prior to the regulation, a 119 criminal year old code was in place, placing stringent restrictions on pregnancy terminations. Prior to this overturn, pregnancy termination was considered a crime under sections 82-84 of the Crimes Act 1900. Under the new terms, women within 22 weeks of conception are permitted to receive an abortion.

CANADA

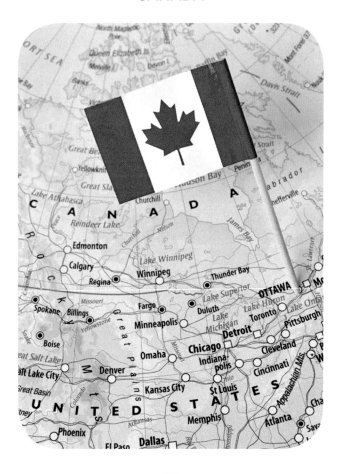

Between 1700 and the early 1800s, abortion prior to 20 weeks after conception was legal in the British North American colonies. However, in the Malicious Shooting or Stabbing Act 1803, performing, or accomplishing to an abortion was accompanied by the death penalty. The death penalty clause was then removed by the Offences Against the Person Act 1837. In 1869, abortion was legally banned, this legislation officially continued in the Criminal Code until 1969.

In 1969, Canada's governing powers declared abortion permissible, but under one specified condition; a certified board of doctors had to provide official confirmation that the mother's life was in danger. Once confirmed, the termination could only be performed in a hospital.

In 1988, the Supreme Court of Canada overturned the country's abortion laws. This was due in large part to the Queen Elizabeth Charter of Rights and Freedoms, established in 1982 and officially incorporated into the Constitution of Canada. The legislation protects political and civil rights to the citizens of Canada, including a woman's right to "life, liberty and security of person."

Between 1990 and 1991, Bill C-34 was introduced by the federal government. This specific bill penalized any doctor performing abortions with a jail sentence of two years. This jurisdiction did not include abortions strictly performed out of risk to a woman's health. The House of Commons passed the bill. However, it was denied by the Senate in a tie vote.

Canada was met with haste between 2006 and 2015. Such bills was the Unborn Victims of Crime Act and The Protection of Pregnant women and their Preborn Children Act were presented to the House of Commons at this time.

CHINA

Pregnancy termination in China is widely acceptable, within reason. There are very few legal repercussions within the time span of 14 weeks after conception. While there are policies in place, the right to pre-pregnancy healthcare is readily available. Although not as accessible as it once was, during a time when abortion was not only accepted, but incentivized.

In 2015, China restructured its one-child restrictions, allowing couples to bring forth two children into the world, due to concerns of the future of Chinese population.

China originally legalized abortion in 1953, making it one of the first countries to take that monumental step. The National Health Commission stated they would take action toward decreasing potentially terminal restraints against unnecessary abortion.

In 1979, China established its one-child policy. This practice not only promoted abortion, but in some cases forced it upon the mothers who already had one child. Fines and forced sterilization often times accompanied those who violated the policy.

EUROPE

Throughout Europe, the vast majority of countries within its borders permit abortion. Thirty nine of these countries have legalized abortion on requested terms. Finland and the United Kingdom permit abortion under specific social grounds.

The countries that allow abortion on request do not demand any particular reasoning for an abortion. The decision to terminate a pregnancy falls solely in the hands of the pregnant woman. The countries who allow abortion on request are as followed: Albania, Armenia, Austria, Azerbaijan, Belgium, Bosnia and Herzegovina, Bulgaria, Croatia, Cyprus, Czech Republic, Denmark, Estonia, France, Georgia, Germany, Greece, Hungary, Iceland, Ireland, Italy, Latvia, Lithuania, Luxembourg, Republic of Moldova, Montenegro, Netherlands, North Macedonia, Norway, Portugal, Romania, Russian Federation, Servia, Slovak Republic, Slovenia, Spain, Sweden, Switzerland, Turkey, and Ukraine.

Term limits vary throughout most of the countries; some limiting it to 18-24 weeks and others capping it at the first trimester. However, should a pregnant woman encounter an emergency situation, there is often more flexibility to procure an abortion in a number of the aforementioned countries.

The countries of Andorra, Malta and San Marino prohibit abortion altogether. In places like Liechtenstein, abortion is only permitted on two accounts; a woman's life is in danger or sexual harassment was involved.

INDIA

Prior to 1971, abortion was a criminal offense in India, upheld by Section 312 of the Indian Penal Code, established in 1860.

In 1979, India introduced the Medical Termination of Pregnancy Act. This granted women the right to pursue safe abortion resources. The Ministry of Health and Family Welfare states that abortion is permissible if the fetus is terminated within 20 weeks of conception, under the condition that it is approved by a doctor and is rendered by a licensed medical professional at an authorized medical facility. An abortion taken place within twelve weeks may occur under the assessment of one doctor. Any procedure needed to take place after twelve weeks requires permission from two doctors.

The Medical Termination of Pregnancy Amendment Bill was introduced to members of the Indian government on January 29, 2020. The bill then found its way into the hands of the members of Rajya Sabha, a section of the Parliament of India. It eventually passed on March 16, 2021, creating the MTP Amendment Act 2021.

Prior to this act, only married women could obtain an abortion

On Thursday, September 29, 2022, the Indian Supreme Court took great strides in accomplishing a new ruling that's being praised as a monumental step toward improving women's rights. This ruling declared that all women, not just those who are married and cis- gendered, are granted equal rights when it comes to abortion. Given that India is populated by 73 million single women, this new ruling provides inclusivity that was non-existent prior to this jurisdiction.

In July 2022, a 25 year old, 22 weeks pregnant single woman petitioned the court for the right to receive an abortion, She had initially sought out the approval from the Delhi High Court, but was rejected. The father of her unborn child had no intention of marrying her, which would have left her to be a single parent. Not only would being single mother with a child conceived out of wedlock bring forth harsh judgements and societal provocation, she was also unemployed with no financial income to support a child. The young woman also raised concern for her mental health should she be forced to bring a child into this world on her own.

LATIN AMERICA

Prohibitive abortion rights have long been embedded in Latin American and Caribbean histories. Similar to other countries with strict abortion laws, women have sought out other alternatives toward obtaining an abortion. Between 1990-1994, approximately 4.4. million abortions were performed within Latin America and the Caribbean. 2010-2014 saw an increase in these numbers, raising the number of abortions to 6.5 million. Many of these procedures occurred under hazardous conditions, leading to thousands of deaths as a direct result.

Latin America used to have one of the harshest bans on reproductive rights, encompassing its many countries and their surrounding islands. In several countries, abortion has been banned in its entirety, with little to no exceptions except life-threatening conditions a mother could face. This draconian form of legislation, if defied, led to stringent consequences, which did not take into consideration the pregnant woman's situation, including if the pregnancy was a result of rape. Mexico could sentence a woman up to 50 years in jail, while in El Salvadore a woman could have faced up to 40 years of incarceration.

Roman Catholicism is the dominant religion reigning throughout Latin America. The religion's staunch viewpoint on abortion has played a defining role in the bans enforced in the countries in which the religion encompasses.

On September 7, 2020, women's rights activists throughout Latin America came together in their respective countries to fight for fair abortion rights. Up until this point, approximately 97% of women in these countries were met with strict abortion regulations. By December of 2020, Argentina.

RUSSIA

Russia's stance on abortion has fluctuated over the past hundred years. When the Bolsheviks took over the country in 1917, the Russian Soviet Republic allowed Russia to become the first country in the modern age to legalize abortion under any circumstance.

Prior to the Bolsheviks' takeover, abortion was punishable by death during Tsar Alexis Romanov's reign. During this time, an underground abortion black market existed, ran and, who were medically trained mid wives who performed the procedures. Between 1909 and 1914, the number of abortions that took place in Moscow more than doubled in volume. At this time, doctors were campaigning for stronger reproductive rights and easier access to contraception.

On July 5, 1921, the Bolsheviks, through the Decree of Women's Healthcare, legalized abortion with the Russian Soviet Federative Socialist Republic. This legislation spread to the rest of the Soviet Union. However, by 1924, restrictions were placed on reproductive rights, allowing only those pregnancies that endangered the lives of the mother or unborn child to be terminated.

Soviet officials began to discuss the strong possibility of women seeking out abortion, even under the thick veil of secrecy. In order to maintain safe abortion practices, officials made strides toward regulating it under legalization. As a result by 1925, nearly 75% of abortions in Moscow were performed in licensed medical facilities. Abortions were made available to any woman seeking one and were often given without any significant cost.

On June 27, 1936, the Central Executive Committee of the Soviet Union introduced Decree on the Prohibition of Abortions, the Improvement of Material Aid to Women in Childbirth, the Establishment of State Assistance to Parents of Large Families, and the Extension of the Network of Lying-in-Homes, Nursery Schools, and Kindergartens, the Tightening of Criminal Punishment for the Non-payment of Alimony, and on Certain Modifications of Divorce Legislation. While this decree encompassed a wide array of legislation, it also deemed abortion illegal once more. This was due in large part toward their desire to accelerate population growth. During this time, abortion rates were increasingly high, with an approximated 4,000 deaths a year from unsafe abortions.

Over the past 20 years, Russia has experienced a decline in population. This has led to stricter abortion regulations. I law was passed in 2011 by Russian Parliament prohibiting abortion after twelve weeks, with the exception of rape, which can be performed up to 22 weeks.

According to Criminal Code of Russia (article 123) states the performance of an abortion by a person who does not have a medical degree and specialized training is punishable by fine of up to 800,000 RUB; by a fine worth up to 8 months of the convicted's income; by community service from 100 to 240 hours; or by a jail term of 1 to 2 years. In cases when the illegal abortion resulted in the death of the pregnant woman, or caused significant harm to her health, the convicted faces a jail term of up to 5 years..

Chapter Irony XIII

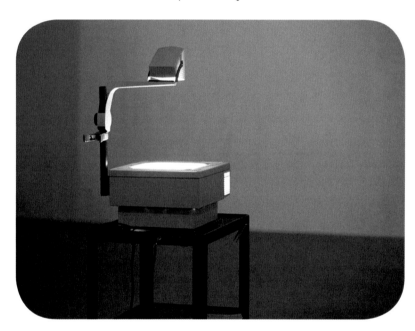

When I was in high school, there was a woman who would come to our school once a year to educate the students on the perils of abortion; deeming such a despicable act as one that would catapult any woman who would partake in such sin into the bitter depths of Hell. She would come into the school with her overhead projectors and outdated movies in tow, gearing up to push her religious agenda on an unsuspecting sea of adolescents.

Moving forward in my life, I experienced a teenage pregnancy at 17 years old. Although being impregnated during the vulnerable teenage years is not ideal, I was content with this pregnancy, giving birth to my adorable and incredible son soon after I turned 18 years old. Although things hadn't worked out with his father, that little boy became my everything.

A few years after my son was born, I had moved on as a single mother. In a turn of events, I had received a phone call from the son of the same woman who would come to my school to spout her anti-abortion propaganda. As it turned out, my former high school classmate had always been intrigued by me and was interested in possibly pursuing a romantic relationship. I immediately took him up on the offer, as he was handsome and super nice.

It wasn't long into dating that he expressed interest in formally introducing me to his mother. I was honored that given the short time we had been casually dating, that he thought so highly of me to invite me to meet his mother. Although I had resided in a small town, word had not gotten around to her that I was the single mother with a great job, and a beautiful heart that her son had been courting.

The day came one afternoon to meet his mother. As I approached her to introduce myself to her, the expression on her face said it all. In that moment, she realized that her "Golden Boy" had taken interest in a young, single mother out of wed-lock. There's was no doubt in my mind that she immediately recognized me. I swear the temperature in the room dropped to freezing in the middle of the summer.

When I attempted to ease the situation, I complemented her on her beautiful dining room table, that of which looked like it was straight out of the medieval castle. It was stunning. My genuine compliment was then proceeded by a very sarcastic, borderline nasty comment. I believe this woman thought less of me for being a teenage mother and preferred her son have nothing to do with me. It also came across so judgmental because I was actually a great mom with a great job and a lot of ambition. I was definitely not looking for a man to take care of me! Even though that happened before I went into business, it was always my dream to be an entrepreneur.

Embarrassment consumed me. It became clear that there wasn't a thing I could say or do to this woman to win her over. She had made her mind up about me the moment I stepped through the door. She wrongly judged me because I was a young single mother who chose to bring my baby into this world, which she had taught me was the right thing to do for all those years.

During this entire interaction, my friend stood there like a deer in the headlights, his face beet red. For obvious reasons we didn't stay much longer. Before we were even finished getting out of the driveway, my date began profusely apologizing for what had happened. Of course I wasn't upset with him. It wasn't his fault.

The genuine sincerity in his voice reassured me that he himself was truly sorry for what had just transpired. I had the preconceived notion that his mother would have had the utmost respect for me for choosing to keep my baby instead of aborting it which was never a question to begin with! She didn't even give me the opportunity to talk about my experience and how the day my son was born was the happiest day of my life. He was my miracle.

It turned out all OK. He and I discussed the situation and decided that it would just be better off if we just accepted the situation and remain friends. I wish he and his family all of the best.

CHAPTER XIV

Forgiveness

FORGIVENESS.

Amongst all of the topics that I have addressed in this book, my intention for writing about this subject was not only because of the Roe Vs Wade changing dynamics for women but also for inner peace, deeper understanding and to comfort those who may not have ever had access to a spiritual opinion in order to comfort their souls. I would have wound up at some point in my life writing this book, regardless of what happened with the Roe V. Wade law. I actually had another book that I was working on and nearly ready to publish when all of this came about. Because of my experiences, I thought that this would be a great time to stop the other book and address and share my experiences with the public. I hope that everyone reading this book has read it with an open mind, and please understand that I have no malevolent intent by publishing this information.

I actually just spoke with one of my dear friends the other day about submitting the book, and how I was nervous about how well the public would receive a book of this nature. My sweet friend said "Susan I have already talked to several of my friends that have had to make decisions like this and told them about your book and they are already asking for signed copies. I also did a Google search on the percentage of the global population that are supportive of abortion being legal I did get varying percentages from different sources, but it seem to be on a regular basis that more than 70% of the population believe that abortion should be legal and a persons own choice having rights over their own body.

Our divine essence, no matter what that means to you, is always a source of complete unconditional love. If any of you, men or women are out there struggling; emotionally physically, or spiritually from guilt because of having a choice that would obviously be a very difficult choice to make. Please forgive yourself, the soul of your child already has, understands and loves you.

FOOTNOTES

Wikipedia

ReproductiveRights.org (Center for Reproductive Rights), Who.Int (World Health Organization),

PRB.org (Population Reference Bureau), american.edu

https://nwlc.org abortion section of website

New York Times article By Dani Blum and Nicole Stock

Updated June 8, 2022 updated June 8, 2022, 5:05 a.m. ET

Amnesty.org (Amnesty International) and PBS Council on Foreign Nations. olwomen.com

www.healthline.com

Contraception and Abortion from the Ancient World to the Renaissance Author: John M Riddle american.edu Articles who will be impacted & Roe vs Wade has been overturned what will happen now. Who will be effected article

https://www.ansirh.org/research/ongoing/turnaway-study https://www.medicalnewstoday.com/articles/sudden-infant-death-syndromes

Read more at Gardening Know How: Cattails In The Kitchen – Tips For Using Edible Parts Of A Cattail

https://www.gardeningknowhow.com/ornamental/water-plants/cattails/edible-parts-of-cattail.htm

New York Times article By Dani Blum and Nicole StockUpdated June 8, 2022 updated June 8, 2022, 5:05 a.m. ET https://w.youtube.com/watch?v=fyiXGW1Mwtw 61435 (pg 53 of this book)

ReproductiveRights.org (Center for Reproductive Rights), Who.Int (World Health Organization),

PRB.org (Population Reference Bureau), Amnesty.org (Amnesty International) and

PBS Council on Foreign Nations. I used those resources for every country.

New York Times article By Dani Blum and Nicole Stock Updated June 8, 2022 updated June 8, 2022, 5:05 a.m. ET

https://nwlc.org/ issue/abortion/

https://www.medicalnewstoday.com/articles/sudden-infant-death-syndrome

americanedu.org & https://www.ansirh.org/research/ongoing/turnaway-study

Wikipedia https://en.wikipedia.org/wiki/Third_eye

https://www.american.edu/cas/news/roe-v-wade-overturned-what-it-means-whatsnext.cfm

Printed in the United States
by Baker & Taylor Publisher Services